# Endorsements

I have often referred to Adhesive Arachnoiditis as "God's Own Disease". It is a disease of great harm, deviousness and loneliness. It creates a feeling of helplessness, hopelessness and fear. Elaine Ballard and "The Furnace of Fire" penetrates the veil of despair that this disease brings to its unfortunate victims. Readers, whether you have the disease of not, will develop an understanding of it, and the need of the victim and family to seek and find spiritual guidance. This book is critical at this point in time because the triad of an aging population, high prevalence of spine diseases, and risky medical interventions have resulted in thousands of cases of which some are now in every community. It is no longer a rare disease. "The Furnace of Fire" points us in a direction to begin the prevention and treatment of this "Devil's Disease". All interested parties should read this most timely and insightful book.

Best wishes always,

**Forest Tennant M.D., Dr. P.H.**, Author of over 300 scientific articles and books, Editor Emeritus of Practical Pain Management

*******

Elaine's book, "The Furnace of Fire" is the first book by a patient for patients on Arachnoiditis. She does an in-depth, articulate and amazing job of sharing what it's like to live with Arachnoiditis and providing hope and motivation for others facing this challenging disease and the pain that goes with it. She teaches the reader how to use mindfulness and spirituality to overcome challenges of living with pain through the strength of faith in Christ. Her faith is a testament to all who live with Arachnoiditis and other chronic pain diseases.

**Barby Ingle** President of International Pain Foundation (iPain), Amazon Bestselling Author and Reality TV Personality.

\*\*\*\*\*\*\*

Actively listening to my patients own personal experiences as well as their opinions on alternative therapies based on their own research, has been incredibly valuable in helping me to become a better physician and a more effective team member in assisting them on their healing journey.

Patients and their families are learning to use online resources to seek out new and creative solutions to problems that have not been addressed adequately by traditional medicine. The ability to take personal responsibility for one's own medical care, although a frightening prospect to many traditional physicians, will ultimately lead to a better quality of healthcare and a more productive relationship between the patient and physician.

Elaine Ballard is one of those individuals who continues to seek out creative solutions to her debilitating disease and reminds us of the importance of recognizing and dealing with the psychological and spiritual effects of chronic pain and illness for those suffering and their loved ones. "The Furnace of Fire" represents Elaine's tremendous efforts to utilize the combined resources of traditional medicine, social media support groups, and non-traditional medical services to better understand her disease and to utilize that knowledge to reach out to others suffering in silence.

Arachnoiditis is a disease that first and foremost should be preventable. Educating Physicians and patients alike is the first step in creating the dialogue towards a better understanding of the disease and to creating better solutions for the treatment of spinal disease in an effort to avoid Arachnoiditis. For those already suffering, Elaine presents many alternative views on traditional care and very useful tips for the patient and their family for taking a more active role in their search for relief.

**Todd K Malan MD**, Founder and Chief Scientific Officer at The Center for Regenerative Cell Medicine, Scottsdale, Arizona
MyStemCellTherapy.com

*******

Since joining our support group, Arachnoiditis Together We Fight in 2015, Elaine Ballard has been a great encouragement and support through her many prayers to so many of our members. Her new book, "The Furnace of Fire" dedicated to those who suffer with Arachnoiditis, is sure to be of great comfort and support to family and friends of those who suffer with this incurable disease. I, as well as many others, will always be grateful to Elaine for her unconditional love, support, and devotion in helping us all make it through "The Furnace of Fire" we know as Arachnoiditis.

**Donna Corley** Pain Patient Advocate, Director of ASAP (Arachnoiditis Society for Awareness and Prevention) & Arachnoiditis Together We Fight

*******

I first met Elaine in the support group, Arachnoiditis Together We Fight. Over the years she has been consistently reaching out to other patients with Arachnoiditis in spite of her own challenges with chronic pain and physical limitations. She is a huge inspiration to myself and to many others who suffer with this incurable disease. I have watched Elaine reach out to patients who have lost all hope and the will to live. Her encouragement and compassion have, I believe, brought much needed hope to so many.

This is the first book about Arachnoiditis of this kind. I believe it will help patients with both Arachnoiditis and Adhesive Arachnoiditis (AA) to know they are not alone and a better life filled with purpose can be found. Elaine's writing style is transparent of her own life allowing others to have a sense of personal connection with the author.

**Michell Freeman** iPain Delegate, International Pain Foundation Your Power of Pain Headquarters

**THIS BOOK IS DEDICATED TO**

The families of loved ones who lost their lives to Adhesive Arachnoiditis. When pain is unbearable, treatment not known or accepted, no cure and faith tested beyond ability to endure, for many it is difficult to find hope.

# THE FURNACE OF FIRE

(Arachnoiditis an aggressive neurological
Disease of the spinal cord)

## FAITH IN THE MIDDLE
## OF BURNING FLAMES

## ACKNOWLEDGEMENTS

I am nothing without God. He has allowed me the privilege of sharing a little in Christ's sufferings and any inspiration in writing this book has come from God's Holy Spirit.

I wish to thank the following friends and Sisters in Christ. Nancy Kriskovich especially, has encouraged me to write this book capturing my own experiences with Adhesive Arachnoiditis and the spiritual lessons I have learned through this journey. Without her support, I would not have found the strength in God to persevere and complete the book.

Donna Corley and Michell Freeman are great advocates of Arachnoiditis and many other related conditions. I truly admire their full time commitment in spreading awareness and encouragement to so many sufferers to keep going when their hope has faded.

Beth Turnbull-Haley and Theodora Fitusis Batisatos are amazing ladies who work tirelessly as Administrators in Support Groups advising, encouraging and welcoming so many members.

I am very blessed to know these five wonderful ladies who continually inspire me with the way they persevere through such devastating and challenging circumstances of their own, and still find time to encourage so many. They are true warriors of Arachnoiditis.

# CONTENTS

Arachnoiditis --------------------------------------------------------9

1. Complete trust -------------------------------------------------11
2. God understands our pain ------------------------------13
3. That special place ------------------------------------------15
4. The priceless value of knowing Christ ---------------18
5. Who are you listening to? -----------------------------21
6. A reason to hope ------------------------------------------23
7. Christ identifies with us ------------------------------26
8. Sacrifice of praise ----------------------------------------29
9. The eye of the storm -----------------------------------31
10. What are you settling for? ---------------------------33
11. Have you met Jesus Christ? -------------------------36
12. God knows what he is doing -----------------------39
13. Be specific -------------------------------------------------41
14. The King of Love -----------------------------------------44
15. How beautiful are your cracks? ------------------47
16. The Devil is after you -----------------------------------50
17. Opportunity for great joy ---------------------------52
18. Are you in a wilderness? -----------------------------55
19. When things go wrong -------------------------------58
20. Our prayers are heard --------------------------------61
21. Raging flares and changes ------------------------64
22. Feeling overwhelmed? ----------------------------67
23. Fed up waiting? ------------------------------------------70
24. Why was I born? ----------------------------------------72
25. The privileged life --------------------------------------76
26. Horrid awful circumstances ---------------------78
27. The unexpected storm --------------------------------80
28. Signs and wonders...1 -----------------------------82
29. Are you willing to suffer?...2 ------------------------85
30. Body and Spirit...3 -------------------------------------88
31. Angelic tree...4 ------------------------------------------92
32. Mind over matter -----------------------------------------95

33. You can't be serious? ----------------------------------------------98
34. Controlling your pain…1 ---------------------------------------101
35. Gifts and distractions…2 ------------------------------------104
36. God's word ------------------------------------------------------------107
37. Fear or Trust? ----------------------------------------------------110
38. Anger ------------------------------------------------------------------114
39. Feeling Guilty? ------------------------------------------------------117
40. Alone or lonely? ---------------------------------------------------120
41. God is faithful --------------------------------------------------------123
42. Why pray? -------------------------------------------------------------125
43. Joy is not lack of trouble ------------------------------------128
44. God's grace ------------------------------------------------------------131
45. Where is peace? ---------------------------------------------------134
46. God knew before you did -------------------------------------136
47. You must forgive…1 ------------------------------------------138
48. Forgive yourself…2 --------------------------------------------142
49. Is suicide a way out? ----------------------------------------145
50. The crown of life ------------------------------------------------150
51. And finally… ---------------------------------------------------------154
52. New bodies ------------------------------------------------------------157
53. Encouragements in the furnace of fire. --------------------159

## ARACHNOIDITIS

Arachnoiditis is listed as a rare neurological condition but in fact many thousands of people all over the world have been diagnosed with it. There are also thousands of other people who have the same symptoms, but as yet, no diagnosis. It is difficult for patients to get diagnosed as doctors are not trained to recognize this disease and often fail to even recognize the symptoms on the MRI Scans.

Arachnoiditis results from severe inflammation of the arachnoid membrane that surrounds the nerves of the spinal cord. It may cause stinging and burning pain, muscle cramps and spasms. The most common symptom is pain which can be severe to unbearable neurological pain especially to the nerves connecting to the lower back, legs, and feet. It can eventually lead to tingling, numbness, weakness and severe pain in the legs and feet. Unfortunately for many, it may result in paralysis. Other symptoms include sensations that may feel like insects crawling on the skin or water trickling down the legs. Severe shooting pains can be similar to electric shock sensations, muscle cramps, spasms and uncontrollable twitching. It can often affect the bladder, bowel, and/or sexual dysfunction. As this disease progresses, the symptoms can become more severe or even permanent. Most people with Arachnoiditis are eventually unable to work and suffer significant disability because they are in constant pain. Pain is the most dominant factor which can disable many parts of the body. It is both chronic and acute. As the disease progresses, the pain can be relentless and unbearable for many and sadly suicide becomes an option.

There are a few causes of Arachnoiditis. Inflammation of the arachnoid can lead to the formation of scar tissue which may cause the spinal nerves to clump together and eventually adhere to the lining wall of the Dura (middle layer of the spine). The disease has then progressed to Adhesive Arachnoiditis. In the 1970's the dye used in myelograms was injected directly into the area surrounding the spinal cord and nerves. The dye was proved too toxic for these delicate parts of the spine and was blamed for causing the disease. This dye continues to be used in some parts of the world and for thousands of more people their lives will be changed forever. Epidural steroid injections may cause Arachnoiditis as well. Chronic compression of spinal nerves can also cause chronic degenerative disc disease or advanced spinal stenosis (narrowing of the spinal column). Infections by bacteria or viruses may also affect the spine. Lastly, complications from spinal surgery or other invasive spinal procedures, including multiple lumbar (lower back) punctures, may contribute to developing this disease. There is no cure for Arachnoiditis and little effective pain relief. This is a disease or condition for life although life expectancy is often shortened a little.

Opioids are offered by doctors but are not specific to reducing neurological pain of this nature. More research needs to be done and doctors trained. It is very sad and cruel that opioids are being clamped down upon in America and Arachnoiditis patients are being classed together with people who seek drugs for recreational purposes. Our voice needs to be heard that we are not drug seekers but desperate victims crying out for something that will stop this relentless overwhelming neurological pain.

## COMPLETE TRUST

*Not a hair on their heads were singed, their clothing was not scorched. They didn't even smell of smoke. Daniel 3:27 NLT*

Trust is complete and utter dependence upon God to do what he has promised even when our situation appears hopeless. King Nebuchadnezzar had Shadrach, Meshach and Abednego thrown into a furnace of fire so hot that his own soldiers died from the excessive heat. These three men of God chose to worship their God rather than worship King Nebuchadnezzar. But look how God saved them? Their hair was not singed neither their clothing scorched. They didn't even smell of smoke! Notice God didn't spare them from this dire situation but gave them inner peace and strength to believe He would work it out for their good and for his glory. The king saw a fourth person in the furnace with them and accepted only their God could have saved them.

Sometimes it seems as if God has put us in a furnace of fire as well! The heat is turned up as we try to cope with burning and agonizing pain that seems unbearable. Electric shocks, brain fog and feeling like an alien in the foggy cotton woolly world around us is truly scary, especially when our legs become numb, weak and paralysis sets in. The burning leaves deep scars as the flames consume our bodies. There is no denying we are indeed attacked and burned in the fiery furnace of Arachnoiditis. But what about our spirit? Can we come out of each flare without any smoke or depression contaminating us? Can we hold on to Gods promise of never leaving nor forsaking us? Do we really believe we can know inner peace while the storm rages around us?

YES, WE CAN, because God loves us deeply and has promised to bring us safely through these trials. He holds us tightly and wipes our tears away as our bodies burn with such intense pain. The question is simple: Do we believe God keeps his promises or he cannot be trusted to do so? The choice is ours to make. We may collect a few scars along our journey but if we continually trust God to cause them to work together for our good, (Romans 8:28), then he will be glorified in our lives and other Arachnoiditis warriors will be encouraged to keep going on their journey. We are all in this together and we need one another.

**PRAYER**
Father God, help us hold on to your promises while in the fiery trials. May we be strengthened in our faith and bring you glory in all we go through. Amen.

## GOD UNDERSTANDS OUR PAIN

*This High Priest of ours understands our weaknesses, for he faced all of the same testings we do, yet he did not sin.   Hebrews 4:15 NLT*

Sometimes I think about the kind of life Jesus Christ had from childhood right up to the Crucifixion. It was far from perfect as he suffered rejection from family, friends, and angry crowds as his friends deserted him. He was also in agony of mind and spirit as he prayed and thought ahead of the unfair trial, dreadful scourging and crucifixion as nails were hammered into his bleeding body. It was so agonizing because he knew he was to carry the heavy burden of all our sin on his shoulders. Jesus also went into hell to defeat the enemy so we didn't have to go there but live in heaven with our beloved Savior. His sacrifice gave us eternal life and forgiveness of sins. Jesus Christ, the Son of God, suffered much more than we can ever do. What love! What sacrifice! What pain he suffered!

When the world was first created it seemed we should have unbroken fellowship with God. The entry of sin changed everything. The way back came through the sufferings of Christ but did not include taking suffering out of this world. God is well able to heal, but he often uses suffering for our growth and his glory.  By acknowledging our own suffering and offering it up to God, we are allowing Jesus to reveal himself in us as the One who suffered. He was man as well as God; therefore he is well able to understand every nerve pain, chronic pain, muscle spasm, every complication and injustice. He understands when we feel like giving up...when it seems too much to endure! He is not oblivious to what the cost is to us. Every time we cry out to him, he will give us the grace to bear these heavy burdens. Just as he was ministered to, so he will minister to us! And remember......after the Cross and suffering came the Resurrection when God raised his beloved Son in power and great glory!

**PRAYER**
Lord, we are grateful you suffered so much on our behalf. Help us to remember the price you paid when we feel overwhelmed by the pain we have to bear. Amen.

## THAT SPECIAL PLACE

*He will cover you with his feathers. He will shelter you with his wings. His faithful promises are your armor and protection.*
*Psalm 91:4 NLT*

Do you remember going to the seaside and finding a little cove or small isolated beach and you were the only person there? Or perhaps a favorite quiet spot anywhere that you longed to go to away from the pressures of this world? We all need to be quiet where we feel at rest, completely secure and at peace. In our busy and noisy world, it is very hard to find such a place. We may spend all year waiting for our holidays when we finally take 2 weeks of rest and pleasure. But as soon as we drive there, unpack, and take in all the beauty around us, it's time to come home again.

Wouldn't it be amazing to live permanently in that special place where it's peaceful and we have time to breathe and appreciate the stillness and beauty there? Pain would be far less as we relax and not dwell on negatives. Well there is such a place....a place of shelter from the storms of life....a place under the shelter of God's wings. There we are covered and protected by his feathers. If we can be still long enough, we will rest securely in Him, letting go of fear, pain and worry. It's there in that secret place we find security because we have surrendered ourselves to his loving, warm and tender care. It's a challenge to remain in that special place but essential for having peace and rest in our hearts all the time. Allow Father God to draw you into his presence and bask in his deep love and care.

I wrote this poem one day as I remembered the struggle of early depression and guilt on my journey in discovering God's rest.

## THAT SPECIAL PLACE

I never thought my Savior would lead me
Down this road of endless pain
I thought He loved me and life would be good
Not filled with heartache and shamefully lame

I hadn't counted the cost of suffering
And what it would mean for me
My life was broken, my heart ripped in two
Crushed, I cried out, "Lord is this really you?"

I fought him in deepest depression
Weary, but so very bold
Break me! Mold me! Make me like Jesus!
Life must have purpose, make the pain pure gold!

He then drew me close, so tenderly
Where I knew I always wanted to be
It was that Special Place where I felt his embrace
And His grace became sufficient for me

He drew me further into his love
Child, there are treasures in store
Stay in the Special Place, you will win this race
And my glory will shine through you more.

**PRAYER**

Father, thank you we can come into your presence where we can rest, feel secure and surrender everything to you. A place of protection from the painful storms of life raging within our bodies. We praise you for this safe harbor. Amen.

## THE PRICELESS VALUE OF KNOWING CHRIST

*I want to know Christ and experience the mighty power that raised him from the dead. I want to suffer with him, sharing in his death....*
*Philippians 3:19 NLT*

Do we really? Do we truly want to have the same kind of power in our lives Jesus had? The kind of power that raised him from the dead? I would suggest most Christians would say they wanted this. Surely, we want our prayers to be powerful and see great answers? We want our family and friends saved into the Kingdom of God. As we serve God using the gifts he has given us, our hearts long to see fruit and success in all we do. In our scripture, today Paul links God's mighty power with suffering. God's Kingdom is not like the world's success. Paul says he wants to KNOW Christ and the best way to do this is through sharing in his sufferings.

This is not for the light hearted Christian. If we keep questioning God about our situations he has allowed, we will never go on to knowing him in a deeper way. Has God made a mistake in allowing us to have Arachnoiditis? A spinal cord condition that causes such unrelenting chronic pain? Pain that can get so dire, some days we cannot even get out of bed! Does he really love us? It's a simple decision we have to make. God is in complete control or he is not! He can't be in control one day, then another day when our pain is bad, say he isn't in control. God never changes and he is faithful. It costs time to delve into our bibles every day so we can hear God speaking intimately into our hearts. Have we been secretly blaming God for this disease and change in our lives? Do we resent him, after all he is meant to be in control? If we have been blaming God then we need to repent and ask for forgiveness. If we don't do this we will gradually move away from his presence in no time at all.

I believe God can and still does heal our bodies. I spent two years asking for healing from my church and was anointed with oil as well. The whole church prayed so faithfully and yet I was not healed physically. It wasn't lack of faith it was simply God had other plans. As I asked about my future and new painful life of disability and what good was I now, God continued to change me from the inside and I began to understand my character and soul were more important to him than giving me a new body. It was through the acceptance of suffering and working with his Holy Spirit, I realized I was KNOWING God in a totally different way. Once I realized how weak I was without him, the more time I spent in worship, getting closer than before and a great longing grew to know him better. So, began a more fruitful life of prayer and writing, the two gifts God was feeding and maturing while in the middle of suffering.

Not every Christian is willing to accept that suffering may come from God. But in this acceptance comes peace and a willingness to say, not my will but yours be done! I have found that in seeking to know God in the suffering, I have discovered suffering can be cleansing and powerful. God can trust me more to put his power within and empower the gifts he put inside me at birth. We can either fight the suffering and try and cope with feelings of bitterness and depression or we can surrender to God in the suffering and ask him to use it to change us inside and bring us closer to himself. The gifts and talents we all have been given will then be more powerfully used and more effective. It will be God's power working through us and not our own human feeble efforts. We cannot have the mighty resurrection power of God without sharing in some of Christ's sufferings. It's in the suffering we recognize our need of God more and this drives us into his presence and complete surrender of our lives.

**PRAYER**
Lord God, you sent Jesus, your beloved Son, into our world knowing he would suffer so much. Help us to surrender our own suffering and trust you to empower us and bring us closer to yourself! Amen.

## WHO ARE YOU LISTENING TO?

*My sheep listen to my voice; I know them and they follow me.*
*John 10:27 NLT*

As I write, the last couple of months have been difficult as my right leg became very numb, weak, and also burning pain covered the entire leg. It was quite a shock as these symptoms came on very quickly and affected my walking. My gait was different and could no longer take the usual normal steps. They became shorter more like shuffling and I could only raise my leg a little off the floor. Then suddenly my left leg started down the same road. I knew then my days of making the three-minute walk to the main lounge was over. Gone were the days of joining in activities with the rest of the residents. The shock of making more adjustments in my already narrow life were quite devastating.

I had two thoughts in my head, one was negative and one was positive. The negative tried to envelop my thinking and told me I would be confined to bed without any help at all. As I tried to imagine how I could get to the bathroom and bedroom, also getting my frozen meals cooked in the microwave, see to my meds, and then wash up afterwards, was all too much and too complicated to even contemplate. I had tried to get care support before but the agencies were either full or way too expensive. I did pray about it all and managed to leave it at the foot of the cross and wait and see exactly how God would act for me. But the negative thoughts became so strong I couldn't bear it any longer. I missed God's peace so I cried out asking him to free me of this negativity. I needed to take my trust in Almighty God to a new level. We cannot serve two masters. We cannot listen to two voices which will only cause confusion and depression. So, I put on my spiritual armor and prayed against the enemy in Jesus Name and by the blood of the lamb! Immediately, the darkness disappeared and trusting God became my priority and Father gave me the faith to believe he was in control. That same day God pointed me in the direction of another care agency willing to provide helpers and the next day both my legs worked better and the pain was much less. Jesus Christ is the good Shepherd and he will do everything and anything to keep his lambs safe and secure. He knows Satan prowls around just waiting to attack, even in our thinking. As Christian we need to know God so well that we recognize his voice especially in the heat of the battle. Then follow our Shepherd and trust him to guide us along the narrow and rugged path that leads to victory.

**PRAYER**
Father, God, forgive us when we don't listen to your voice and we allow the enemy to lead us into misery and depression. Help us to know your voice more clearly and to trust you. Amen.

## A REASON TO HOPE

*The soldiers gave Jesus wine mixed with bitter gall, but when he had tasted it, he refused to drink it. Matthew 27:34 NLT*

I want to try and bring a message of HOPE today. Our lives are full of challenges which at times seem too hard to cope with. With the withdrawal of opioids for many, I do realize it has been the tip of the iceberg and many question whether they can go on. I had a fall two days ago which upset the nerve/Arachnoiditis part of my body. I feel weary, in dreadful pain and wonder if my semi paralyzed legs will deteriorate further. So, what should we do? Give up and stop fighting or can we find that little spark again to ignite our determination to carry on trusting God? Can we find a little hope so we don't bring enormous pain and suffering to our loved ones by opting out?

Friends, we are the fore runners for thousands of other Arachnoiditis sufferers to come. They are waiting in the wings, as yet undiagnosed, but one day they will be given this diagnosis, and like us, they will be bewildered and lost! And the cycle will continue. We are in a position to understand and reach out of ourselves and work together; using whatever talents we have to move forward in finding a cure and spreading awareness.

I was challenged by the fact Jesus refused to drink from the sponge that was mixed with sour wine and gall. It would have lessened the cruel and agonizing pain of the Cross. The reason why Jesus refused to drink was because it contained something that would dull the pain he was about to endure. It was a compassionate gesture but Jesus knew He had to FEEL every pain and suffering known to us even today. The Crucifixion was the cruelest pain possible. Refusing the drink was like refusing the opioid that would nullify the pain. Jesus was committed to suffer even more than we do, so we could kneel before the Cross and say like him…

*"Father, if you are willing, take this cup from me; yet not my will, but yours be done." Luke 22:42 NIV*

By saying this we are leaving all our pain and suffering at the Cross and allowing the Son of God bear all our suffering. In return, we are given forgiveness for our sins, strength to carry on and an inner joy that doesn't go up and down with our circumstances. The choice is ours. His outstretched nailed hands torn into shreds and bleeding and broken body carried everything we cannot carry. The Savior of the world died and suffered outrageous pain just for us. Surely, we can carry on in his strength with our burdens rolled away. We still might have the pain, or not, but we can be renewed within to keep moving forwards. I know some of our lives are dreadfully hard but there is a Source of help who understands completely because he didn't give up, such was his love for us all.

**PRAYER**

Thank you, Lord, for taking upon yourself our suffering and pain. You didn't give up when all of hell raged against you. Please help us to never give up but to live in the strength and resurrection power of the Cross. Amen.

## CHRIST IDENTIFIES WITH US

*And when you believed in Christ, he identified you as his own....*
*Ephesians 1:13 NLT*

Sometimes when God wants to reveal something that will have a deep impact in our lives; he chooses to do it in a supernatural way.

I was lying on my bed in the living room as usual, when in the middle of my devotions I felt the urge to look up. My eyes rested on the beautiful picture hanging on the wall in front of me. I loved it because of the old thick broken branches lying on the ground and the gnarled trunk looking the worse for wear. The stream of flowing water to one side added magnificently to the scene. The picture was full of character but as I gazed in front of me I only saw one thing. A perfect 3D image of the face of Jesus! It was deeply scarred and blood trickled down the side of his face. A crown of thorns lay deeply embedded into his forehead. The color of his face was a mixture of brown, red and yellow from the blood, sweat, tears and dirt mingled together running down his face. His hair was not neatly combed. No, it was matted, straw like and dirty. My dear Savior's face was in deep agony of pain and suffering and I cried... and still shed tears every time I look at this picture. This revelation was given to me 16 years ago and it is still there today.

You would think all this was enough to give me a deeper and clearer insight into the sufferings of Christ. But there was more and perhaps this one thing had the greatest impact on me. Jesus

Christ, the Son of God who sits at the right hand of the Father, and who has all power and authority, was lying on the ground ON HIS SIDE! He was IDENTIFYING with me! I cannot lie on my back or front and now need help to walk. My legs are continually in severe pain and are numb, weak and the nerves tremble all the time. Conventional medicine does not touch this type of nerve pain and for many Arachnoiditis sufferers, this is what we have to cope with day after day without care and help from our doctors who generally do not understand this disease.

Christ's sufferings are incredible enough but to actually see him lying on his side, identifying with me, made me understand the importance of Christ suffering every detail of our suffering. God needed him to go through everything we as human beings have to, and without sinning. This was the only way Christ could become the Spotless Lamb and be the perfect sacrifice for our sins. So friends, never think you are alone and no one understands your unique circumstances. God knows exactly how hard we are trying to cope and he sees every tear that has trickled down our faces. Remember God loves us so deeply he intended his Son to go through everything we have to. This means he understands what we are all going through right now. Don't allow the pain or your circumstances to depress you and think God doesn't care. He is right there beside you, holding out his hand, eager to embrace you. Allow him to hold you tightly and feel his power, strength and healing flowing into your body.

## PRAYER

Lord, how can we express our thanks for going through your own sufferings so you could identify with ours. We are so grateful and ask you to forgive us when our faith has been weak. Amen.

## SACRIFICE OF PRAISE

*Therefore, let us offer through Jesus a continual sacrifice of praise to God, proclaiming our allegiance to his name.   Hebrews 13:15 NLT*

How often do we think of praising God while in the middle of a storm or valley? When our day goes wrong or just feeling down, it's so easy to feel sorry for ourselves and wish things were different. But our emotions and situations CAN change if we will stop and simply gaze at our Almighty and Sovereign God! Shifting our focus from the problem to God and praising him for no other reason than he is awesome, faithful and trustworthy, aligns our spirit with His and we are drawn more closely to him. It's called the sacrifice of praise because it is a sacrifice. It costs us something when we choose not to be fed by our fallen nature. I believe God honors this kind of praise, and as he is lifted up, so our hearts are renewed and faith restored in God who is well able to guide us safely through the fire.

But what does a 'continual sacrifice of praise' mean? We are all human and have to learn how to keep our negative emotions in check. There is a place we can reach where we can still stay calm in this furnace of fire. Of course, it's easier to express joy and enthusiasm when appropriate but when pain hits us like burning flames, what happens to our thinking and emotions?

Life is full of choices and it's our responsibility to choose how we react. I find it hard to pray out aloud during intense pain. Talking seems to use up energy I haven't got. But I know if I allow my mind and thoughts to stay with the pain, the day is wasted and I feel I have accomplished absolutely nothing. The continual sacrifice of praise means to disregard how we are feeling all the time and make that hard choice to tell God how much we love him even though it might mean praising him with our thoughts. God is well able to hear us and this is something that comes with practice. The more we do it, the more it becomes our 'norm' to praise him come what may.

As Christians praising God should be a natural process. We should long to worship the Risen Lord and King of Kings! We should never be happier than when we are in his presence. It is while we abandon ourselves to our beautiful Savior, his healing power moves upon us and the flames are extinguished and we are at peace again. Praise God!

**PRAYER**
Loving Savior, help us to be consistent in our reactions to pain. You are worthy of continual praise. Teach us how to worship you through the fire until all our days become a sacrifice of praise.  Amen.

## THE EYE OF THE STORM

*Suddenly, a fierce storm struck the lake, with waves breaking into the boat. But Jesus was sleeping.  Matthew 8:24 NLT*

Last night as I lay in bed trying to sleep, I began thinking about hurricanes. I used to love extreme weather in winter, especially thunderstorms and high winds but as long as I was indoors looking out! I saw the high winds swirling around and the storm powerfully picking up cars and trucks, scooping them into the air as they were carried upwards, then violently dropped to the ground. These hurricanes can cause so much damage. They are full of ferocious power that can leave us gasping at their intensity! Life can be the same. Suddenly, we may feel the onslaught of problems too heavy for us to handle and we have no idea what to do. But in the center of a hurricane, is a place of safety called The Eye of the Storm. The problems and intense storms are still raging but they are moving around the center. It's called the Eye Wall. The Wall is protecting the Eye, the place of safety. Nothing can harm us if we are in the center where it's all calm. So, it is with God. He is always at the center of the storm where it is calm and very peaceful. He wants us to stay with him right there in the Eye of the Storm. He has made a special place of safety if we will rest in Him. We need to totally trust God who not only made the wind and rain but also made a place of safety for us right in the center of the storm. So, storms may come into our lives but they need not harm us because God remains in the center, providing all the shelter we need.

Jesus was sleeping in the middle of a fierce storm. Even as the pounding waves were breaking into the boat, he still kept on sleeping! How could he manage to do this? Perhaps he wanted to demonstrate faith and God's miraculous powers to his disciples? Maybe he wanted them to see for themselves that to fear is to sin. Trust and fear cannot go together. These disciples would certainly never forget this lesson.

*"Suddenly, a fierce storm struck the lake, with waves breaking into the boat. But Jesus was sleeping. The disciples went and woke him up, shouting, "Lord, save us! We're going to drown!""* Matthew 8:24-25 NLT

Arachnoiditis is a cruel disease that can test not only our bodies but our faith as well. How are you doing on this journey? We need to stay close to the Lord, read the bible each day, listen to hear what the Holy Spirit is saying and pray. As we do these things we will be bathed in the beautiful aroma of his deep cleansing peace that will cancel out all fear. We might see and hear the raging flames still trying to ravage us, but if we stay close to Jesus in the center of the storm, the furnace of fire cannot harm us.

**PRAYER**
Mighty Savior, we want to stay so close to you that these fiery storms do not control our thinking and emotions. Draw us closely to yourself where there is peace and quiet rest. Amen.

## WHAT ARE YOU SETTLING FOR?

*Plow up the hard ground of your hearts, for now is the time to seek the Lord, that he may come and shower righteousness upon you.    Hosea 10:12 NLT*

Are we looking at what God can do for us or seeking an intimate trusting relationship with Jesus Christ? Sometimes the joy and infilling of the Holy Spirit as we decide to follow Christ is exciting. We come to understand our sins are forgiven and we are filled with love so deep and pure, perhaps for the first time, we know we are accepted just as we are. I still remember my own conversion and how it totally changed my life.

After a period of time God allows Satan to attack and tempt us back to our old natural lives. It is often very subtle and if we are not careful, we make a wrong decision which may lead to other wrong decisions. Or perhaps we get too complacent and stop reading our bibles every day and find little time to pray. After all, life is so busy these days. While we may change, God does not. He created us with one purpose only and that was to have an intimate loving relationship with him. God is love; he doesn't just give out love, He IS love! That is why he created us to share in his deep, free, and eternal love. God longed for this kind of loving friendship but didn't want us to be robots. He created us with an empty space in our hearts that can only be filled with him. We have free wills which gives us the choice to enjoy God or put ourselves first and only give him a fleeting glance.

Has the difficult long journey with Arachnoiditis gnawed away at your heart? Has the relentless pain or medical harm pushed out your first love? How many more flare-ups can you take? Life has changed, friends made their excuses, spouses unable to cope. The list is endless for this disease can cripple our bodies until we cry out in despair and depression! However far we may have run from Jesus and filled that empty space with something else, there comes a time when we have to make a choice. Repent and return to our first love or embrace all the negativity, anger and guilt that comes from our experiences of burning in the furnace of fire. We may cry out to God for help, extra strength or even healing and continually feel disappointed for not finding what we need.

Which is the better way? Depression, anxiety, thoughts of suicide, feeling useless or walking daily with Jesus in intimate fellowship, love, and hope? One way will satisfy and bring meaning to your life while the other leads to despair. If you have moved away from Jesus Christ then return fully to him. Commit your health and all the difficulties to Christ for he is calling you back. None of us can cope with Arachnoiditis or any serious chronic pain illness on our own. It is simply, too much! We were not meant to cope in our own strength. Stop looking for answers. We will not see or understand fully this side of heaven. Accept that you are loved. You are treasured. You are a Child of Almighty God. You are Royalty. You are a Royal Priesthood. You are the Bride of Christ. You are so highly thought of that Jesus Christ suffered and died on the cross just for you! You are forgiven! Return to where you belong....in the loving arms of your Savior where peace, strength, joy, and hope will be found!

**PRAYER**

Renew our hearts Lord and forgive us for moving away from you. Help us to make the right choices and return to your loving arms. Amen.

## HAVE YOU MET JESUS CHRIST?

*For this is how God loved the world: He gave his one and only Son, so that everyone who believes in him will not perish but have eternal life. John 3:16 NLT*

Are you reading these devotions and finding some of them hard to understand? While we are outside of Christ we can't see things clearly because our minds have not been renewed by the Holy Spirit. But when we actually invite Jesus into our lives to take full control, it's then the veil is removed and we see everything through the mind of Christ. It's an amazing thing to suddenly understand the bible better and our lives begin to make more sense. Of course, learning is a gradual process that will be with us for the rest of our natural lives. We should never stop reading the bible asking the Holy Spirit to open our understanding of God's Word. We never stop learning.

There is no fear in love and God didn't send Jesus into the world to condemn us. No, we actually stood condemned to hell by our own choice by refusing to accept the Risen Lord as our Savior. Our sins condemned us before but the moment we ask for forgiveness and accept Jesus Christ as the Son of God, forgiveness flows freely. You are loved and cherished and God wants to welcome you into his Kingdom to receive love, mercy, hope and grace to accomplish his will in our lives.

I have often wondered how people who are not committed to the Lord, cope with chronic pain, especially Arachnoiditis. The pain is relentless and often acute. Where do they get enough strength to help them get through this cruel disease? It seems to me the more consistently vocal people are in their complaining, I see an enormous amount of anger coming from within them. Anger can energize us but it doesn't produce inner peace, only turmoil which creates more physical and mental pain. We can have anger at the medical profession for not being willing to help support us. Anger with friends or family not able to understand this disease. Anger at losing our former lives. So much anger, regret, disappointment and loss!

So, as Christians, how should we handle this? We are all human and share these same emotions. The difference is we have direct access to our Heavenly Father who tells us to ask him for anything and he will do it. We have stepped into a readymade family and have become children of God. Prayer is our access and we should be praying or talking to God at any time day or night. The Holy Spirit also intercedes for us especially when we find it hard to pray. So, the anger we may also feel doesn't have to stay inside poisoning our bodies and making us worse. God releases his love, compassion and mercy as we surrender these negative attitudes to him.

*"And he who searches our hearts knows the mind of the Spirit, because the Spirit intercedes for God's people in accordance with the will of God." Romans 8:27 NIV*

There have been many times when God has calmed the flames in my body as I have known his healing hand upon me. But even when, in his wisdom he withholds healing, his grace is always available so we can lay the anger at his feet and accept his bountiful grace to forgive and carry on in the midst of the storm.

**PRAYER**

Thank you Lord for our salvation and your promise to never leave or forsake us. We praise you for your glorious grace that keeps us strong when we are so weak. Amen.

## GOD KNOWS WHAT HE IS DOING

*My thoughts are nothing like your thoughts, says the Lord. And my ways are far beyond anything you could imagine. For just as the heavens are higher than the earth, so my ways are higher than your ways and my thoughts higher than your thoughts. Isaiah 55:8-9 NLT*

If you had the choice and power to improve your life, how would you change it? What would you leave behind? What would you include? What treats would you give yourself? Who would you surround yourself with? Our imaginations could, I am sure, prove overwhelming at the amazing life we could give ourselves, a life without problems or illness and disease. A life filled with joy, happiness, peace and laughter! What an idyllic life we would choose for ourselves.

However, our lives are not like that and we have to face up to the reality of believing God's promises and his Word. We are to live by faith, *"For we live by believing and not by seeing."* 2 *Corinthians 5:7 NLT*. In other words, we have to believe that God knows the whole picture and will always be working on our behalf for our good. We may not actually see the good for a long time, sometimes we may never see it this side of heaven. But if God's ways are indeed higher than our understanding, we have to accept what is happening, will indeed work out for our good. Isaiah 55:8-9 says that God's ways are beyond anything we could imagine! So, it's a waste of precious energy and mental torture trying to understand. God is God! We are not God! We are his creation so how can we question God like Job did?

Perhaps one day when it's time to be called to our heavenly home, we will be allowed to see the reason WHY? I am sure our questions will be answered and we will actually see the whole picture. We will finally understand and regret how we sometimes denied Almighty God of our trust, respect, and honor.

God created everything to be perfect. I am sure walking in the Garden of Eden together with the Lord, as Adam and Eve did, was absolutely amazing. Think of the wonderful fellowship they would have had? But when sin entered this perfect world, everything was tarnished and we lost the perfection of beauty around us. Our thinking was affected as well as we became self-centered rather than God centered. That is the nature of sin.

We need Almighty God to change our perspective. We need the Holy Spirit to convict us and we need our beloved Savior to heal our hurting and often angry hearts. We need to look up away from ourselves and see God reigning from his Throne. We need to repent and surrender everything to him. We need to trust him big time just because he is GOD.

*"Just as you cannot understand the path of the wind or the mystery of a tiny baby growing in its mother's womb, so you cannot understand the activity of God, who does all things." Ecclesiastes 11:5 NLT*

**PRAYER**
Lord God, we ask forgiveness for not accepting your ways are higher than ours. Forgive us the anger and frustration we feel at times and forgive us when we have exalted our knowledge above yours. Amen.

## BE SPECIFIC

*I am exhausted from crying for help; my throat is parched. My eyes are swollen with weeping, waiting for my God to help me.*
*Psalm 69:3 NLT*

In the above verse; it appears David had been crying out to God for a long time. He was in such depths of sorrow, his continual weeping exhausted him, made his eyes extremely swollen and he was miserable while waiting for God to help him. Perhaps some of us have been in a similar situation where we have cried out for help to the Lord and there has been silence. Our kind of pain can be unrelenting and out of control and I know personally our minds can become hazy. In these times voicing our prayers and making them specific, is hard. These days I sometimes pray without voicing my requests simply because I have little energy to spare and so I pray in my mind.

However, the Lord challenged me a little while ago to pray out loud when I can. Hearing how we are praying and what we are asking for has more impact on us. In my experience, shouting out my frustrations to the Creator, brings out the real agony in my soul. It releases pent up feelings and I believe God listens more intently because our prayers are coming straight from our hearts.

The other part God challenged me to do was to stop asking for his help. The word 'help' is so general. I do recognize there are sometimes situations where we don't have time to go into detail and 'help' is all we can say. God understands this. But to only ask for help when we do have more time is not really asking God for exactly what we need. In this verse Paul says he prays about you and your needs to God.

*"God knows how often I pray for you. Day and night I bring you and your needs in prayer to God....." Romans 1:9 NLT*

He is praying specifically for the needs of the Christians in Rome. There is no hint that he is praying just for help. He prays for their 'needs'.

Sometimes we pray for people and ask God to 'help' them. Then move on to the next person on our list and ask God to 'help' them too. It's a lazy and easy way to pray. God wants to hear how we are coping with our loss of our old life or the increase in pain or how we feel about a certain person. Of course, he already knows but needs to hear from us. God loves us and in his love, he longs to communicate, to have a two-way conversation. It's so easy to cry out or say, 'help me' but when we pray from our hearts about a certain situation either for ourselves or for someone else, God wants to see and hear our emotions and attitudes. I do believe our Creator answers these kinds of prayers because he created us and knows how important it is to pray from the heart. He also wants to speak into the situation we are praying for. We need to give him time to speak as well for us to pray effectively.

**PRAYER**

Lord, help us to pray from our hearts and tell you how we are really feeling. Speak to us while we are listening. Amen.

## THE KING OF LOVE

*We know how much God loves us, and we have put our trust in his love. God is love, and all who live in love live in God, and God lives in them.  1 John 4:16 NLT*

Every morning in my quiet time I do a few things. One is to read the next hymn or song from a Song Book. I sometimes find nuggets of gold that were hidden from me many years ago. This morning I read, "The King of Love my Shepherd is whose goodness faileth never....." A very well known and loved hymn. But I couldn't get past the first line...The KING OF LOVE.....!

Jesus has many titles. When we think of an earthly king or even a president or leader of a country, we imagine he has a kingdom or country that he is head of and he has a great responsibility to govern and provide for. But they all rule differently and may make mistakes and an issue of trust arises. Jesus Christ is the King of LOVE. He has a Kingdom but he left it to bring Kingdom LOVE to us here on earth. He brought us Kingdom love so we might understand a new way of living our lives and interact with people in the purest and deepest form of love there is. Because Jesus is the KING of Love, there can be no other who can love us as he can and does. We need not be afraid to open our hearts and invite the purest form of love to come right in. The King of Love cannot fail, make mistakes, or have a day off especially when we need him. '.....I nothing lack if he is mine and he is mine forever!'

Having a chronic disease like Arachnoiditis can bring out our negative side if we are not careful. Our lives may be filled with rejection from doctors, health experts, some friends or family. I know how hard this has been for me over the years. I have lost many people from my life and now find myself living alone without any medical help or friendship. It's a bit scary and if it wasn't for the lessons I have learned, over the years, to trust God's word and to remember all the many times he has come through for me, I would have caved in a long time ago. We have to deal with a great deal of rejection and it can make us very negative. I find people are far more eager to talk about the negative rather than focus on the positive. While we cannot ignore these negative feelings, we must deal with them before they consume us.

The King of LOVE is the Kingdom of Heaven. There will be no room for our negative thoughts there. So, we must acknowledge the hurt in our hearts and ask God for forgiveness. I know it doesn't seem fair we have had to suffer medical harm without much support. But there is no reason we can't fight to make Arachnoiditis more aware and pray for a cure. Our attitude is very important. God will not hear our prayers unless we are filled with Kingdom love and have sought forgiveness. Leave the unfairness and medical harm in God's hands.

*"Dear friends, never take revenge. Leave that to the righteous anger of God. For the Scriptures say, "I will take revenge; I will pay them back," says the Lord. Instead, "If your enemies are hungry, feed them. If they are thirsty, give them something to drink. In doing this, you will heap burning coals of shame on their heads." Don't let evil conquer you, but conquer evil by doing good." Romans 12:19-21 NLT*

**PRAYER**
Forgive us, Father, for holding onto negative thoughts against people who have let us down. Fill us again with Kingdom Love so we might be at one with our precious Savior, the King of Love.  Amen.

## HOW BEAUTIFUL ARE YOUR CRACKS?

*How foolish can you be? He is the Potter, and he is certainly greater than you, the clay! Should the created thing say of the one who made it, "He didn't make me"? Does a jar ever say, "The potter who made me is stupid"? Isaiah 29:16 NLT*

God is the Potter who created us. He made us because he is Love and love always is a driving force that longs to reach out to everyone. He longs to have fellowship with us for that is what love is all about. God lovingly created us to be unique from each other. He has a specific plan and the gifts we have been given are to equip us to carry out that plan as we journey through this life.

So, what goes wrong when we find ourselves changing? Maybe life itself with all its obstacles, health, hurts and failures, take hold of us and we are not careful to react in the right way. Or perhaps we get treated badly but never truly forgive others or ourselves. These unresolved issues may form cracks in our character or personality. They may cause depression and the light and love of our Creator, grows dimmer as darkness begins to take over. It is essential we keep a record of how we are feeling or recognize these cracks and seek God to remold us into his image again.

God is always keen to bring inner healing to everyone who asks. It takes courage to stop and rest in God's presence, knowing there is something the Holy Spirit is nudging us about!

But when we do surrender and listen, we will not only be confronted with the sin but also entirely soaked in the most anointing and cleansing love of God!

Inner healing is beautiful but sometimes costly. We will be forgiven, cleansed and closer to Jesus than ever before. But we will have cracks where the bad memories have been as well as the hurts. These cracks, however, do not have to be a negative. Inner healing fills up those cracks with gold because we overcame by the blood of the Lamb! That means we are even more beautiful than before! The golden scars or cracks will always be there this side of heaven because they are there to remind us how God loved us so much he sent Jesus to die in our place on the cross. We are loved that much and so much more! Sometimes I am reminded of mistakes or fears I had in my early years but marvel at the way God has radically changed me into who I am today. He shows us the cracks because he wants to heal them. He wants us to be freed from the consequences of sin and gradually become more like Jesus. These scars are very precious as well as beautiful because they represent the times we fought to become an overcomer! They also remind us how we can help and encourage others who are struggling, for we now have experience of God's grace soldered into the cracks and we and they our priceless!

Never say no when God turns the heat up. If we do, we will only struggle and hurt more. Refining is a wonderful humbling experience and as the layers of mold and dirt are chipped away, we begin to be a better reflection of Jesus than before. We can trust what the Potter is doing. He is qualified to chip away and it will only be as painful as we let it. What pours out of our mouths and heart, might surprise us. But God wasn't taken by surprise, he knows us better than we know ourselves and wants to change us to become more like his Son, Jesus Christ. Allow God to reshape you on his Potter's wheel. See these trials as an opportunity to grow rather than fight them. If you fight God all the time you will grow weary and give up. There is always a reason for each trial.

**PRAYER**
Thank you, Father, for always pursuing us so we face these trials and receive inner healing and forgiveness. We want to shine as pure gold in a dark world and reflect your glory! Amen.

## THE DEVIL IS AFTER YOU!

*So humble yourselves before God. Resist the devil, and he will flee from you. Come close to God, and God will come close to you.*
*James 4:7-8 NLT*

Satan will do everything within his power to bring us down into depression and steal the good life God still intends us to have. If we have committed our lives to God and received Jesus Christ as our Savior, the enemy hates us! He is still trying his best to overthrow Almighty God and take his Throne for himself. Satan is power mad and wants to reign supreme in God's Kingdom. He will stop at nothing to get what he wants and the reason why he hates us is because we have become heirs with Christ Jesus and will inherit the Kingdom. We are his enemy and are in his way so he will not stop attacking us, especially in our weakest moments. It's when we are unhappy and fighting against God's will that Satan attacks. At first we may not recognize our minds and thoughts are being very subtly attacked and that is why we should always be ready and aware of his schemes.

It would be so easy to give in and feel sorry for ourselves because we are victims of medical harm. How dreadful! So we begin to feel righteous and hard done by and in so doing move away from the Lord. We might not recognize this at first but as this scripture says,

*"Stay alert! Watch out for your great enemy, the devil. He prowls around like a roaring lion, looking for someone to devour."*
*1 Peter 5:8 NLT*

He is watching our every move and decision we make and when we give in, he sees an opening and starts to devour us!

Spiritual warfare is very real and we must always wear God's armor to protect ourselves. If our mind is attacked then put the helmet of salvation back on. Protect our minds at all costs. The helmet will prevent the enemy from infiltrating our thoughts and tempting us to feel discontented with our lives. The next step will be blaming God, and eventually we are convinced he doesn't care. The devil wants to devour our allegiance to Father God. That is his aim and if we start to lose our joy and peace and trust in God, then we become depressed and are giving the enemy a foothold into our lives. Friends, we must fight with our spiritual armor on and our eyes upon the Lord. He has promised to never leave us and still has that good life planned ahead. Trust him in these hard days and years.

**PRAYER**
We ask you, Lord, to help us be alert of Satan's attacks. Renew our hope as we come closer to you. Amen.

## OPPORTUNITY FOR GREAT JOY

*When troubles of any kind come your way, consider it an opportunity
for great joy. For you know that when your faith is tested, your
endurance has a chance to grow. James1:2-3 NLT*

When we read or think about this particular scripture, we tend
to feel a little uncomfortable for how can troubles ever bring us
great joy? After all, we are either happy or sad; we never believe
we can feel both at the same time. How can it be? It certainly is a
difficult thing to understand.

The deep inner joy that never leaves us can only be found from
having an intimate relationship with Jesus Christ. So how do we
get to know Jesus in this way? Going to church and listening to
sermons is great but it is not a substitute for spending quality
time in God's word and then wait in the silence to allow the
Holy Spirit to speak into our hearts. As we spend this precious
time with Jesus each day we are getting to know him better and
our inner life is being cleansed as he reveals sin that perhaps we
have forgotten or didn't think was so bad at the time. God does
not want to punish us but he does want to have deep fellowship
with us. After all, that is why he created us. The talents he gives
us are tools to help accomplish his plan in our lives. He doesn't
expect us to carry out this calling without equipping us to do it
well.

So, as we get to know the Lord better, we will change more into
his likeness. This process of knowing Jesus better should be the
desire for the whole of our lives. Through good and bad, we

should never stop spending personal time together and confessing our sin. This is how we develop a deep joy in the Lord. The joy of knowing someone so intimately brings us freedom too.

When I first met my husband, it was love at first sight and neither of us wanted to be away from the other. We met together whenever we possibly could and enjoyed each other's company so much. He even stopped having evening meals so he could spend more time with me. I seem to remember he lost over a stone before we married and he never told me why! The more we shared so our love deepened and the joy of knowing each other grew more. But that joy could only come from spending time together. We should be longing to be with Jesus just like engaged couples long to be together. Some Christians call it 'first love' but there is no reason why it has to fade. I know our lives can change through situations or bad health but that 'first love' with our Savior, should flourish and deepen during these difficult times.

Our joy should not depend on our circumstances, however unjust and awful they may be. At the first sign of a problem we should be rushing into God telling him all about it. Then reading the bible asking the Holy Spirit to speak into the situation. That's how we keep our joy in the Lord. Simply trusting Him to guide us through the flames and to bring his purposes out from it. Jesus Christ is totally trustworthy and has a reason for allowing these trials we face. If we keep our first love fresh and continually be in his sweet presence, we will hear his voice, the voice we have come to love, and experience his all-encompassing compassion and strength. He will walk with us THROUGH the furnace of fire and we will not get burned!

**PRAYER**

Our Father, forgive us when we stopped spending quality time with you and lost the joy we had. Take us back to our 'first love'. Amen.

## ARE YOU IN A WILDERNESS?

*The Spirit then compelled Jesus to go into the wilderness, where he was tempted by Satan for forty days. He was out among the wild animals, and angels took care of him.  Mark 1:12-13 NLT*

We all, at some time, find ourselves a little low or depressed and God's presence seems to have disappeared. We read our bibles and try to pray but God is silent. It is a crucial time when our faith is tested. Jesus was led into an actual desert where it was hot, deserted, no other people and he had no food to eat. He stayed there for forty days aware of wild animals stalking him for a juicy meal. The verse above says the Spirit compelled Jesus to go into the wilderness. He was led there. So, from this we can understand being in a dry place is not always because we have sinned but it can be a test from God. We must take heart and believe we will come through these difficult times. Jesus was protected from harm by the angels and God will also protect and guide us until our time of testing is finished.

Why does God want to test us? Jesus was led into the desert straight after his baptism when God declared he was well pleased with his Son. So often, after we have been in a special place of blessing, God does test us to enlarge our faith. Jesus had to go through this wilderness to affirm his obedience and faith, to listen to what God was saying and to equip him spiritually for his ministry ahead. Father God knew what lay ahead for his Son. He wanted to prepare him and this was how he chose to do it.  We sometimes forget Jesus was human as well as God's Son. So, his humanity had to be tested just as ours are. When God allows these temptations, it is to strengthen our faith and loyalty to him. The wilderness experience is to help us face certain issues in our lives that God wants to strengthen.

During these times God will often draw us to things deep inside that we have buried and never resolved. It might be anger, unforgiveness, pride, envy, hurt or disobedience. Whatever it is we must come to God with an open heart and allow his Spirit to work in a particular area. It isn't a sign of weakness but more a time of growth. Jesus is the True Vine and his Father is the Gardener (John 5:1). He wants to prune every part of us so we become more like Jesus Christ. So instead of protesting over difficult situations, we must rise up and allow the pruning to happen.

Pruning may hurt, we may cry, we may suffer loss of health or friendship. One thing we can be sure of, it will be painful! Real growth doesn't come without stretching, testing our faith, and requiring a deeper commitment. It will be costly. God wants to use us to reach a hurting world. But to be his instruments we must be sharpened and molded into his image. Then God gets all the glory! Never run from these times. God will always pursue us and we will make the journey worse than it needs to be. Even God's dearly beloved Son had to go through testing and many trials. Why should we be surprised when we go through our fiery trials? There is a reason for everything God brings or allows into our lives.

**PRAYER**

Thank you, Lord, for these testing times where we can grow and mature in Christ. Prune us until we are more like Jesus. Amen.

## WHEN THINGS GO WRONG

*Trust in the Lord with all your heart; do not depend on your own understanding. Seek his will in all you do, and he will show you which path to take.   Proverbs 3:5-6 NLT*

If you are like me, you keep a list of things to do for the next day. They may not appear important to others but to us it's our way of coping, making sure we don't make the list too difficult or too long. With this disease, we need to make choices and only do perhaps one thing a day. Afterwards we are exhausted and need time to recover. The extreme chronic pain and burning flares often take all our energy away.

Life is rarely as we would choose and so often we get interruptions from other people's expectations or maybe from our own. How do we cope well with these setbacks? Our scripture today tells us to trust the Lord and to not depend on our own understanding. I believe every interruption is allowed or sent by God. His wisdom is far beyond ours and many times when we don't understand, we have to choose to believe God has a very good purpose.

I love the story in 1Kings about a widow and her son. Life had been very hard for them and they were down to their last meager meal. She had obviously thought about it a great deal and after eating they would prepare themselves for dying. She was out of 'spoons' and all hope! But God interrupted her plans by sending Elijah the prophet. There was a great famine in the land and everyone was hungry. So, when Elijah asked the widow for food she declared....

*"I swear by the Lord your God that I don't have a single piece of bread in the house. And I have only a handful of flour left in the jar and a little cooking oil in the bottom of the jug. I was just gathering a few sticks to cook this last meal, and then my son and I will die."*
*1Kings 17:12 NLT*

At Elijah's insistence, she started to prepare the food. I wonder if she resented this interruption for her important plans. But as she obeyed and didn't follow her feelings, so the food multiplied and there was enough food for very day. Elijah blessed her with this promise...

*"For this is what the Lord, the God of Israel, says: There will always be flour and olive oil left in your containers until the time when the Lord sends rain and the crops grow again!" So, she did as Elijah said, and she and Elijah and her family continued to eat for many days."*
*1 Kings 17:14-15 NLT*

The story doesn't end here. Later on, the widow's son became gravely ill and died. But Elijah was there to pray for the boy and God restored him to life. What an amazing story of what started out to be an interruption of someone's plans that turned into such huge blessings! So, welcome the uninvited guest who suddenly appears or the telephone call you haven't got time for. Even the unsympathetic caller who pops in just when you had planned to lie down and rest. Nothing happens by chance to God's children. He uses the good and not so good to work out his purpose in our lives.

**PRAYER**

Lord, forgive us when we have resented these interruptions. Please help us to see them as possible blessings that you have planned and prepared for us.  Amen.

## OUR PRAYERS ARE HEARD

*And a great amount of incense was given to him to mix with the prayers of God's people as an offering on the gold altar before the throne. The smoke of the incense, mixed with the prayers of God's holy people, ascended up to God from the altar where the angel had poured them out. Revelation 8:3-4 NLT*

Prayer can be difficult to understand when we don't always see the answers for a while, although I do believe God hears them if they come from a clean heart. However, some answers may not come as we expect them to and we wonder why? How many times have we asked God for healing when the flames burn more fiercely? I have known times when God has graciously lessened the pain after praying or others praying for me. In his compassion, he sees how we are struggling and intervenes. That is why it's so important to continually pray and intercede for each other. There have been many occasions when I have asked for prayer and have actually felt the intensity of God's deep healing love around me. That is such a blessing knowing many people are praying and to feel God's hand upon me in a special way.

The Book of Revelations Chapter 8 reveals what happens to our prayers once they are said. It is an amazing picture where angels are present around God's Throne. One particular angel has the task of presenting our prayers before God. He is so very holy while our prayers have been spoken from human hearts and sometimes without much thought. This particular angel mixes our prayers with a huge amount of incense and then the beautiful sweet aroma of prayers and incense is offered up to God!

What a beautiful picture of how our prayers are received. They are not floating around in the sky forgotten and ignored by our loving Father. No, he wants to hear from us. God gives our prayers special treatment that's how much he values our fellowship with him. Of course prayer is part of fellowship as we are talking and perhaps singing our praises to God. Of course, he wants to share with us as well, so we must always listen for his voice. Years ago, before I read these verses I always wondered if an angel carried our prayers to God for us. Then I imagined my prayers were sent directly to him because my sins have been forgiven and I knew I was accepted just as I am.

I believe there is something more here; something not to be missed! Why would God need to have our prayers mixed with incense before he received them? We are sinners, yes, but we are also saved by grace. This appears to be the final act that is recorded just before God sits in judgement on the world. Maybe God is hearing the anguish of his people, all the hurt and wickedness and the many many cries from injustice. These prayers are very special because injustice and hurt from his vulnerable children hurt God too! Keep praying friends, justice will be done in God's good timing.

*"Then the angel filled the incense burner with fire from the altar and threw it down upon the earth; and thunder crashed, lightning flashed, and there was a terrible earthquake." Revelation 8:5 NLT*

**PRAYER**

We praise you Father for hearing every single prayer and when we hurt, you hurt too. Fill us with your love and joy and leave justice in your hands.  Amen.

## RAGING FLARES AND CHANGES

*Don't be afraid, for I am with you. Don't be discouraged, for I am your God. I will strengthen you and help you. I will hold you up with my victorious right hand. Isaiah 41:10 NLT*

A big part of Adhesive Arachnoiditis are the many 'flares' and changes in our condition. We only have to over stretch ourselves a little but it's enough to alert our bodies to react with aggressive inflammation and severe unrelenting pain. It may last a few days, weeks or months. Finally, when the injured nerves and body decides it's all too much, it caves in and never returns to the way it was before the flare.

I believe I have had Adhesive Arachnoiditis symptoms since 1994 when I lost my sitting position and had to lie on my sides all day and night. My confirmed diagnosis came in 2015 and another one in 2017. To begin with, the dreadful spaced out feeling with the outside world in front of my eyes telling me I was an alien, was very strange. The head fog that caused such confusion made me feel inhuman. When the inflammation got out of hand, the flares laid me aside for a couple of weeks. But as the years passed I grew used to it and struggled less. I also learned how to treat inflammation better. Then the tingling began in my toes before numbness entered my feet. At first I ignored it but soon realized this was not going away...ever! Within two months numbness spread all over both legs and feet and the worst pain ever accompanied it. Some days I cannot walk at all. Other days I can shuffle a little but every day around 4pm both legs shut down and refuse to move. The condition is called Allodynia. I try and arrange my meal and tea to fit in before this time. Life has changed dramatically and the neurological pain in both legs and feet is sometimes over bearing and I struggle with feelings of "I've had enough!" Now the time has come for me to decide to have more help where I live or move into a care home. Changes, changes, and yet more adjustments! How can we possibly cope?

I can only share my own experiences of coping through this nightmare but these are times when I have also experienced the most joy and deeper fellowship with Jesus Christ. How can that possibly be? I have been a Christian for 50 years and sometimes it's been very tough. God has taken me through situations that have broken me many times. I have fought to survive and not end my life although I did try a couple of times in the early years. What kept me going was reading God's word no matter how I felt and always being real with My Maker. I remember times of shouting at him, times of sharing my heart and also telling him of my doubts in his ability! One time I was so upset as I thought God couldn't be trusted. I felt I could trust him but how could I trust God if he was not trustworthy? So many things kept going wrong and I was badly served by the medical profession for years. Finally, God did reveal his trustworthiness and healed my broken heart. It came in his time when I was ready.

As I look back on these heartbreaking times, I see very clearly that all the time God was refining me into his image. He had been breaking me so he could remold me even with those beautiful cracks which we know are priceless treasures. I had always longed to reach out and love people but was too frightened of rejection. God broke the shell I was hiding in and used all the bad situations to make me into the person I am today. He has now been able to remove the clutter from my heart and filled me to overflowing with his deep concerning love for others. It's up to us if we allow God to use this disease to refine us or we fight against what God has allowed into our lives. It may not look like it at first but he can use it all if we offer each part up to him.

**PRAYER**
Loving Father, we are amazed at what lengths you go to get our attention. Come and refine us as we give you the struggles we are facing.  Amen.

## FEELING OVERWHELMED

*Do not be afraid, for I have ransomed you. I have called you by name;*
*you are mine. When you go through deep waters, I will be with you.*
*When you go through rivers of difficulty, you will not drown. When*
*you walk through the fire of oppression, you will not be burned up; the*
*flames will not consume you. For I am the Lord, your God, the Holy*
*One of Israel, your Savior.  Isaiah 43:1-3 NLT*

This past week has probably been one of the worst times ever.
My doctor advised me to move into a Care Home as my legs are
rapidly getting weaker with the nerve damage from Adhesive
Arachnoiditis There comes a time around late afternoon when
they seize up and refuse to move. Rapid nerve degeneration of
my legs is scary and hard imagining how I will cope on my
own. My imagination is running overtime as I wonder how I
will get to the bathroom. Can't sit to use a wheelchair and
walking becomes almost impossible. I might have to try
crawling! I found out today Social Services may turn residents
out of their Care Homes when their finances reach a certain
level. One move is enough but a second one when I will be
much worse in health, would be unthinkable.

The present Care Agency I am with is pretty bad. I have had
excellent care givers in the past and mostly they do a great job.
But when care givers are two hours late and the main care giver
doesn't always wear protective gloves before washing me, I
think this is unacceptable. One day, she washed me with dirty
hands and no gloves. Dirty marks left on doors where she had

opened and closed them. Over the years I have found having care givers can bring stress and takes over your life.

My physical energy is very low and runs out quickly. These last few weeks trying to prepare to sell my apartment as well as numerous interviews regarding finances has drained me physically and mentally. It is hard as well trying to find the right Care Home that will accept me and not too expensive. I also need a room on the ground floor which is essential as I can't sit or walk to a lift. I have to do all this and everything else while lying flat. It is almost impossible!

So, what is the answer? I think the question to move and risk being turned out of a Care Home later when my finances run low is my biggest concern. I know I would not be able to face yet another move. I need to trust God for finances to cover the increasing care I need now, and will need in the near future. It's easy to say, "Trust God" but when I am physically overwhelmed how do I relax and trust Him? I am coming to the conclusion that if one road is so overwhelming during the process, if it is drawing me downwards so quickly, then perhaps God is saying this is not the way. Sometimes God wants us to GO THROUGH the storm but if that's right, he will give us all we need to accomplish it. So perhaps I should stay in my present apartment. However, ultimately I want God's will in my life.

When I started on this journey of moving I asked several friends to cover me with prayer. As the intensity of obstacles and stress grew, I shared this with them and asked for more prayer. A couple of hours later a deep peace rose within and I refused to let this peace go. When God is called upon from deep within our hearts, he not only hears but he sends exactly what is needed. I share this experience with you all as I know many have found themselves at the very end of the rope or edge of a high cliff. Surround yourselves with friends who will pray and intercede on your behalf. We cannot get through the horrors of this disease alone. Its limitations and dreadful pain sometimes takes a tight hold and we need each other so much. Hold on friends, our God will guide us away from situations that don't bring his deep peace. He will always provide another way....His way!

**PRAYER**
Thank you Lord for your gift of peace which guides and protects our hearts. We praise you for going THROUGH the flames and for setting us an example of how to keep going when it's tough! Amen.

## FED UP WAITING?

*Commit everything you do to the Lord. Trust him, and he will help you. Psalm 37:5 NLT*

It seems harder to trust God when we are not sure what his will is. Waiting for answers when other people are involved in your future, adds to the difficulty because the human element and advice can be wrong. But I still appreciate advice and will always listen to people who know me. God still has a fruitful plan even for the last part of my life so I must wait quietly and listen to his voice.

Of course, this doesn't mean I stop thinking and weighing everything up. Far from it, I have made lists of pros and cons into moving into a Care Home against staying in my beautiful and comfortable apartment. Yesterday it seemed staying here outweighed the problems of a Care Home. Today, I feel it's best to go into a Care Home. The bottom line is I cannot cope very well living on my own even having care givers in three times a day. So, my mind is weighing up the possibility of finding a Care Home that will meet my needs. It needs to be local so I can still access my doctor who is learning more about Adhesive Arachnoiditis. I still need the community dentist and my present optician to treat me in the home. I would love a good-sized window and nice view as this room will be my home hopefully for the rest of my life. The Lord says,

*"If you believe, you will receive whatever you ask for in prayer." Matthew 21:22 NIV… (So I claim this scripture and wait!).*

Waiting is hard but we must learn to wait patiently, however long God determines it to be. He sees and knows the big picture. He understands our weaknesses and often makes us wait as he knows the lesson will stretch our spirit. Of course, we may have to wait, because the timing is not right. Whatever the reason, waiting will produce a deeper longing to be closer to Jesus and an opportunity to trust him totally. We will experience his love as he ministers through his word and in worship. Of course, this is up to us. We can be impatient and turn our backs on God by not reading the bible or devour the Word. We need to search the scriptures and ask the Lord to speak to us. We need to pray and praise God more just because we love him and not for what we want him to do for us.

Are you in a waiting period as I am? Don't panic or worry, it blocks out God's voice, causes stress and sleepless nights! Let's put on the full armor of God and protect ourselves from the devil's schemes. (Ephesians 6:11-12). Yes, we have an enemy who will attack us the moment we let our guard down and get impatient. God has his reasons for asking us to wait. Let's trust him to prove how faithful and trustworthy he really is.

**PRAYER**
Lord God, forgive our impatience and help us to trust in your perfect will and loving faithfulness. Amen.

## WHY WAS I BORN?

*You made all the delicate, inner parts of my body and knit me together in my mother's womb.....You saw me before I was born. Every day of my life was recorded in your book. Every moment was laid out before a single day had passed. Psalms 139:13, 15 & 16 NLT*

Possibly the two most important days of our lives are when we were born and discovering the reason why?

Have you ever wondered why God created you? Why you were born in a certain part of the country? Did God choose your parents? Is the country and place of birth relevant? In Psalm 139 we learn God made every part of us. He knit us together in our mother's womb. God actually saw you before you were born! These are truly incredible thoughts.

First of all, we can see in these verses that none of us were born by accident. We were not born because our parents didn't use contraceptives or because they didn't plan having us. No, we are not a mistake or accident. Almighty God made all the delicate, inner parts of our bodies and knit us together in our mother's womb. He watched over us as our tiny parts were formed together, and from a fete grew into a baby with hands and feet and even a brain. God, our Creator, must have lovingly watched every stage of our development and loved us unconditionally. We were beautiful, loved and given a purpose, a reason to be born. Every day was recorded in his Book and also each moment of every day was planned before the first day ever took place!

Wow! How can we ever understand this? We were created so lovingly and intricately with a purpose. What was that purpose? God gave us gifts as he designed us. The main purpose was to have fellowship with our Creator. God designed us in such a way we would be longing to reach out and worship him. Worship was to fill us with fulfillment and joy for that desire was created in us by God.

Secondly, we were all born with gifts and talents which are our tools to enable us to do the specific work God planned for us from our conception. We are all different and our gifts are not the same. God's plan was made in perfection but once we started to mature we chose to become independent of God. Sin and rebellion emerged and clouded those gifts and purpose for our lives. It took many many years for me to accept my gifting as I was shy and fearful of authority. I did not excel academically because God gifted me in a creative way. Writing, poetry, drawing, making my own clothes and craft hobbies were hidden away and frowned on as a child and I was forcefully encouraged to push harder in the wrong direction. It was in my 30's when I began to understand the things I was good at, was my calling.

If God went to so much trouble with every detail of our make-up and gave us a purpose with specific gifts, it's not difficult to believe he provided the right people to be in our lives. Even the place where we were born must be significant. God uses everything, the good, the down-right ugly and sinful things in us, as well as our relationships. He uses every detail to refine us as well as sharpening our gifts and talents. All the time, bit by bit, we are growing and coming to understand his purpose.

Perhaps we were in full bloom or just blossoming in that purpose when Arachnoiditis hit us! Boom! We were hit by a sudden brick wall and all our dreams of using our talents disappeared! In my experience, I am finding the academic side which was pushed and expected of me is quite irrelevant now. I did write a lot before including writings songs. But without encouragement, the writing didn't flourish as it could have. Having to deal with growing Arachnoiditis since my accident in 1965 and Adhesive Arachnoiditis for several years, has put me in a position where I have a great deal of experience now to write about. In all the struggles and challenges Adhesive Arachnoiditis brings, God has refined me through them. Now the two have come together and I have confidence to write, as well as experience to pass on to other people.

Don't give up your hopes and dreams. As God removes something, he will always replace or expand it in a different way. So, don't be boxed in with how you think. Expand your imagination and ask God to show you a way whereby he can still use the gifts he put inside when he formed you in your mother's womb. We were born to have fellowship with God and to glorify him by using the gifts he gave us.

**PRAYER**

We praise you, Lord, for creating us in such a special way. Forgive us for being angry at our changed circumstances and seeing only the things we have lost. Renew our vision of these gifts that are still there waiting to be used again. We long to glorify you Lord by using them. Amen.

## THE PRIVILEGED LIFE

*Because of our faith, Christ has brought us into this place of undeserved privilege where we now stand, and we confidently and joyfully look forward to sharing God's glory. Romans 5:2 NLT*

We have so much in our day to day lives that can take away our peace. When our bodies are aggressively raging in pain or we constantly think about the future and what might happen, peace cannot be found! We become what we are thinking and then we can't stop ourselves from being a little bad tempered. To change our mind set takes practice and determination but it can be done. These days I have to deal with pain in both my legs that refuse to lessen, as well as weakness and rapidly increasing numbness. Every day I know I must arrange my time to fit in with the strength in my legs. As said earlier, I tend to reach a peak late afternoon. It's here I have to make a choice. Do I give in to negativity and focus on the 'what if's', or do I commit it all to the Lord? I may not understand why I have to go through certain things...all I know is we live in a fallen world but God is still in control.

God created a perfect world where pain and conflict did not exist but when he created human beings, he gave us power....power to choose how to react. Sin and disease entered the world with Adam and Eve. It was their choice to disobey God and eat an apple which was forbidden. So, generations later, God has still given us the same choice. We know what we should do and how we should react but we count it too hard to bother.

God has not brought disease and sickness upon us, he loves us, but he does expect us to hand everything over to him. As we do, he will pour his strength into our ailing bodies and give us hope as we trust him to use us.

The Christian's life is about reflecting the glory of God to everyone around. The more difficult our journey, the deeper the reflection of God may be seen in us. It's a privileged life but not many will take up the challenge. The choice is ours. What will you choose today?

**PRAYER**
Refine us Lord until we reflect your glory! Complete your work of grace in us until our will becomes one with yours. We dare not count the cost for you chose the nails, the agony of the cross and fierce attacks from the enemy. You went THROUGH the furnace of fire. You overcame so the victory can also be ours. How we praise you, mighty Lord!  Amen.

## HORRID AWFUL CIRCUMSTANCES!

*So, do not throw away this confident trust in the Lord. Remember the great reward it brings you! Patient endurance is what you need now, so that you will continue to do God's will. Then you will receive all that he has promised.  Hebrews 10:35-36 NLT*

I guess when you reach a certain age you can afford the luxury of looking back over the years and think about situations you've been through that changed your life. I think I have needed lots of problems because I can now see how life changing they all were. When we suddenly find ourselves in circumstances that are difficult or even desperate, at first we think we shall never survive the stress that goes with it or the actual difficulty itself! We remember the scriptures that tell us God heals our diseases and He rescues us in times of trouble and the name of Jesus Christ has power to bind the enemy from attacking us! We are well equipped and know how to handle our situation whatever it is. But then, for some reason, it doesn't happen for us and we wonder why?

*""This went on day after day until Paul got so exasperated that he turned and said to the demon within her, "I command you in the name of Jesus Christ to come out of her." And instantly it left her.""*
*Acts of the Apostles 16:18 NLT*

Now, looking back, I can see a little of God's wisdom. If he took away all my problems when I asked him to, I would not have learned perseverance, trust, faith and just how trustworthy He is. It's in the waiting we learn how to trust and mature in our walk with the Lord. Of course, all the attributes mentioned above about God are true. He does heal us, he rescues us and we can call on the name of Jesus Christ and see his power at work in our lives! But it's in the middle of these trials that we learn and mature.

I feel so thankful for past situations God allowed or even brought my way, because I am a totally different person now to how I used to be.
I know for sure, it's been IN the horrid awful circumstances that God changed me and I learned to wait for his timing, not mine!

**PRAYER**
Thank you, Lord, for working all of our circumstances together for our good. Forgive us when we are impatient and remind us that your timing is always perfect. Amen.

## THE UNEXPECTED STORM

*The Lord is good, a strong refuge when trouble comes. He is close to those who trust in him. Nahum 1:7 NLT*

We all have to deal with unexpected problems but we don't like the lessons God wants to teach us through them. It's while we are struggling, we are being stripped back of all that hinders our relationship with God. It may be we are relying more on our job that's well paid than trusting God completely to be our source of supply. If we lost our job could we trust God to still provide for us?

Maybe Jesus wants more of our attention. Have we stopped reading our bibles and rushed through praying. Is our time with him less of a priority than five years ago? Perhaps the Lord wants us to help someone but we are too busy to hear him. There are lots of reasons why we find ourselves in the middle of problems. All of us will go through them. It may not be our fault but God will always either use them to teach us something or to test our faith and trust in him.

Whenever I hear this song I am very encouraged! Knowing Jesus is in the middle of the storm holding my hand and guiding me through the darkness, is so reassuring! Friend, if you are struggling, reach out for the Master's hand, he won't let you go. He is your refuge, your place of safety and will bring so much good from this storm, you will be amazed!

## THE UNEXPECTED STORM
(Composed by Sandy Blythe)

From out of nowhere the blue sky grew dark
And without any warning it seemed your whole world just fell apart
Right now you're wondering does the Master even see.
Does he know where I'm standing? Has he forgotten about me?

For the unexpected storm
It hasn't caught him by surprise
Right now he's watching you
I know he'll bring you through
Safe on the other side
You don't have to be afraid
Through the thunder and the rain
In the shelter of his arms
He'll keep you safe from harm
Through the unexpected storm

Every storm has a reason though it's hard to understand
Every trial has a purpose it's all part of God's plan
Through all of your questions he will never leave your side
But he'll be your refuge until the storm passes by

## PRAYER
Lord Jesus, thank you that every trial has a good purpose and you are right in the middle, holding our hands, strengthening us all the time.  Amen.

## SIGNS AND WONDERS....1

*I want you all to know about the miraculous signs and wonders the Most High God has performed for me. How great are his signs, how powerful his wonders! His kingdom will last forever, his rule through all generations. Daniel 4:1-3 NLT*

Both the Old and New Testaments are full of times God displayed his glory and guidance to his people in signs and wonders. I don't believe he has stopped communicating with us in these special ways. I read books and occasionally hear from other Christians of their experiences but perhaps the signs and wonders are not given to us as frequently or we are not hearing about them so much these days. With the new laws regarding equal rights for everyone, it has become increasingly difficult for Christians to share their faith. I have noticed on several occasions when I do mention God or Jesus in conversation, I am frowned upon and more often ridiculed for being a Christian. So, it's not surprising we don't hear much about signs and wonders!

I don't know why but God has revealed his message to me in the form of these amazing, almost unbelievable signs and wonders quite a few times. The first occasion was at my conversion. I was a shy, withdrawn child who grew up frightened of authority and people. I thought I was a Christian because I lived in a Christian Country. I was searching for love! To be loved and to give love. I felt desperate inside. After seeing a film called Two a Penny, I was handed a form at the door written by the Billy Graham Association. Bored, I filled it in and soon after I posted it, they wrote back and sent me a book called Peace with God. It made me question whether I was a Christian. I thought I was as I lived in a Christian country. But this book and a subsequent visit to the Billy Graham Offices helped me question my faith or lack of.

As I entered my apartment a few days later, there was a bad smell of fish. It seemed strange as I hadn't bought any. Then I felt drawn into the living room and there on the window was an image of the most ugliest face I had ever seen! I knew immediately it was evil and pulled the curtains across to hide it away. But this evil, ugly face shone through the curtains, terrifying me. Then everything suddenly changed. God removed the blind from my eyes and I suddenly understood the book I had been reading about having peace with God. I knew I had to make a choice to break free from the strong grip of Satan and give my life to Jesus Christ. I looked the enemy straight in the face and told him to "go from me!" declaring I loved God and was going to serve him. I knelt down by my bed and said very little except that I wanted to serve him. It was enough because I was then covered in a blanket of deep, pure selfless love. I had never experienced anything like it before. I cried tears of joy and an unbelievable peace entered my soul which has never left me. As I rose to my feet I looked at the window, yes the face of Satan had gone! The next day as I travelled to work on the tube, everything was brighter, more colorful and a new confidence filled me because I knew without any doubt, God loved me and I was brimming over with love for him.

I would like to use the next three devotions to explain other experiences of the supernatural I have been blessed with. Each one has brought spiritual growth and a deeper understanding of the love of God. Now, I am compelled by the Holly Spirit to reach out and tell everyone God brings to me, of his deep, cleansing, all-consuming love whether by word or action. I cannot be silent for our loving God has done so much in my life.

**PRAYER**
Amazing Love, how can it be that you, my God, have died for me! Amen.

# ARE YOU WILLING TO SUFFER? ...2

*I have refined you, but not as silver is refined. Rather, I have refined you in the furnace of suffering. Isaiah 48:10 NLT*

I will never forget listening to Richard Wermbrant speak about the persecuted church in Russia. I arrived in Melbourne, Australia in 1968, a few weeks before and was thoroughly enjoying my new life as a Christian. But this meeting was different to anything I had heard. Richard Wermbrant had been imprisoned for his faith for many years and was now traveling around the world telling of his suffering and torture while in prison. He was trying to educate Christians and challenge us to pray for our brothers and sisters in Christ. It was the first time I had heard about this kind of persecution and decided to pray regularly.

I was quiet on my way home digesting all I heard and went to bed straight away. I was tired and soon fell asleep. A few hours later I suddenly woke up aware of somebody in my room. I should have been scared but I wasn't. There was a very real sense of peace around me and I lay awake for a few minutes soaking in the beautiful atmosphere. I knew it was the presence of my dear Lord, Jesus Christ. I didn't see him but heard his voice very clearly in my heart.

He spoke directly to me asking if I was prepared to suffer for his sake. Of course, I didn't understand what kind of suffering he meant. All that passed through my mind was, I didn't think I would be going to prison for owning a bible as Australia was a Christian country and nothing like that was likely to happen. I felt safe in this great land of sunshine and barbecues and great Christian friends. No, it certainly wasn't going to be that kind of suffering, I thought. But what then? I had no idea what God had in mind but I was sure of one thing, whatever my future held, if suffering was a part of it, I would gladly accept it. He had changed my life and already I could feel the refining process had begun. The shyness and fear of people was gradually getting less and I was beginning to reach out to people with God's love. In my innocence, I said "yes" to the question God asked me.

To this day I remember that question so clearly because God reminded me of my reply in 1994 when I was unable to get off my bed. My husband had to turn me over with a sheet such was the pain and agony of the slightest movement. This lasted a full year as the multi-level disc disease progressed significantly. But this kind of suffering was proving way beyond my ability to endure. As I cried out to God so he reminded me of his question and my answer. All those years ago, God saw this coming but he knew he could heal me deep down like no other way could, and he would be glorified in it if I let go of my fears and questions.

It wasn't easy to still say 'yes' to suffering and allow God to use it. But as I look back now, I see He was a real gentleman for asking my permission to allow me to be refined by this furnace of suffering. He knew it would be hard beyond measure but through it he has been faithful in sustaining me. I needed something so special from God that I would never doubt his goodness in this fiery trial. It has kept me going all these years, in fact it has kept me alive knowing Almighty God revealed his will in this special way. Yes, God still uses signs and wonders even today.

**PRAYER**

Your ways are truly amazing Lord! Thank you for still speaking to us in signs and wonders today. Help us to be open to hear from you in any way you choose. We love you! Amen.

## BODY AND SPIRIT...3

*Yes only God knows whether I was in my body or outside my body. But I do know that I was caught up to paradise and heard things so astounding that they cannot be expressed in words, things no human is allowed to tell. 2 Corinthians 12:3-4 NLT*

We were created with a body, mind, and a spirit. Today some doctors are recognizing the importance of having hope and a purpose in our lives and when these two things are eliminated through sickness, depression can quickly set in. So, the spiritual dimension plays a very significant role in our well-being.

I had emigrated to Australia, settled into a good spirit filled church and joined the choir. Life should have been pretty good but I was feeling low, fighting God, as he found ways of challenging me to move forward in expressing his love. I was still scared and needed to grow deeper in the love of God.

One night as I got into bed and prepared to get off to sleep, the strangest of things happened. I was wide awake; it was no dream, when I felt my spirit rise up out of my body! As I was led upwards by an angel, I thought my head was going to hit the ceiling! It seemed I lowered my head just in time, but really there was no reason to do this as I was in my spirit and not in my physical body. The same thing happened as the roof came into view and my natural reaction was to duck my head again. Then I was led a certain way upwards far above the night sky. Eventually I was directed towards a light where I could see people in the distance. As we grew closer, I was surprised to notice I knew everyone. Some were leaning against a tree reading a book, others were smiling and chatting. It seemed an idyllic scene until I heard words of desperation coming out of their hearts. The smiles and occasional laugh hid the hurt inside each person. "Help me, help me!" was their cry yet all I saw were happy faces.....it confused me!

I wasn't there very long when the angel led me back the same way through the clouds and endless sky. I remember going through the roof and ceiling of my bedroom, I looked down at my bed where my body lay still in the same position as when I left it. I hadn't been aware of any pain or physical limitations but as soon as my spirit returned to its body, so all the pain from recent surgeries and other physical degeneration, returned with abrupt awareness. Yes, my spirit was once again residing in my mortal body!

I lay there quietly trying to make sense of what had happened. In my spirit, I heard God tell me that I wasn't the only one who was scared. Most people had some fear or feelings of desperation or very unhappy with their lives or themselves. They had learned to mask their emotions and only allow people to see their happy, altogether side. Then I realized we were all pretending to be strong. Strong in the Lord and strong in ourselves. Only I wasn't pretending! People could see my vulnerability and I felt their judgement.

A second time, my spirit rose from within my body and I was led up through the ceiling and roof into the sky. That was when the journey changed and the angel bid me follow in the opposite direction. It seemed a long journey but eventually I saw this brilliant light ahead. I felt a deep longing to get there quickly. It was inviting! It was Home! I remember some things that happened but not as much as I wanted to remember. But I shall never forget the incredible experience of being in the presence of Almighty God! It was like being born again only so much more than words can express. My loving Father embraced me so tightly and warmly I never wanted the experience to end. All my tears and fears melted away, and oh the inexpressible joy of being filled with such pure heavenly love was life changing!

I don't remember any streets of gold or pearly gates or any other angelic beings. Only God! I am sure that was his intention because when it was time to leave, he told me I would not remember the awesomeness of being in heaven itself, only what took place between the two of us. Sometimes in the back of my mind, I think I see a little glimpse of heavenly beings. Whatever I did see and experience had an enormous, life changing affect upon me. God had healed me from the fear of rejection and filled my heart with a deep heavenly love. I was now ready to reach out to people. This kind of love compelled me to hurt with the hurting, grieve with the sad and rejoice in the happiness of others. I am not special. I am a simple soul who loves God and has always longed to reach out in love but was never able to until this deep cleansing experience. God knows our needs and the best way to bring healing.

**PRAYER**

Lord, we are so grateful you know exactly how and when to heal us. Please help us to have an open heart to see you in the miraculous as well as in the normal situations of every day. Amen.

## ANGELIC TREE.....4

*What are the angels, then? They are spirits who serve God and are sent by him to help those who are to receive salvation.*
*Hebrews 1:14 GNB*

I have always believed in angels even before I became a Christian and read about them in my bible. The more I read about angels and the ministry God had given them, so my interest grew. I became very aware of the presence of angelic beings protecting me although I didn't see them with my eyes, I instinctively knew in my spirit.

As I lie on my bed in the living room I have a good view of some beautiful trees. They are all in a garden opposite me and I love to look at the tall oak tree with its large trunk and thick over hanging branches. Next to it are two delicate ash trees. The thinner branches bear a mass of light green leaves grazing the ever changing sky. I love this view and when the squirrels run across the lane to quickly access the safety of the trees, it's such a delight watching them. All kinds of garden birds nest and sing their little hearts out in them. I am truly blessed to have such an interesting and beautiful part of God's creation nearby.

It was winter; the green leaves had faded into shades of red and yellow and finally fallen down. The cold had set in and I felt sorry for the birds having to work hard searching for worms or any pickings they could find. I didn't normally spend a lot of time just gazing at these trees, but one day as I looked up from my bed, I saw an outline of an angel in the oak tree. Two thinner branches had entwined together to form a head. Two long arms were open wide as if embracing me. This image of two open long arms was very powerful as they seemed to be reaching out to my home where I lived; assuring me I was being guarded, watched and lovingly protected. God revealed this image about a year ago, and every day I look for my guardian angel! He is there all the time and even when the leaves grow on the branches in the summer; his arms are so long I can still see them.

Having this image of an angel in a tree overlooking my home has made me constantly aware of God's goodness and the lengths he will go to communicate with us. God knows us better than we know ourselves, he understands how best to communicate and exactly what we need to see and hear. I live on my own now and at times I admit I feel a little insecure when things go wrong. Before, I relied on my husband, now I am much closer to God because I need him to be my help mate, my source of protection. This has given me a deep awareness that I am being watched and loved. I truly am able to live in peace because God has communicated his protective presence over me.

Again, I say, I am not special! I am a child of God just like you. So, look for signs and wonders your Heavenly Father has already designed for you. Open your eyes as you look at his beautiful creation and also look at the everyday, ordinary things of your life. It seems he loves to use the things that we are interested in to reveal himself to us! Now, that is amazing love isn't it?

**PRAYER**

How we praise you, Father God, for being so creative in communicating with us. Open our hearts and eyes to see the precious notes you leave for us to find. We love you! Amen.

## MIND OVER MATTER

*.... let God transform you into a new person by changing the way you think. Then you will learn to know God's will for you, which is good and pleasing and perfect. Romans 12:2 NLT*

Pain is pain, right? The kind of pain we have from Arachnoiditis is chronic and at times acute. It is the same for other people who suffer with chronic pain whatever the name of the disease. Every day we have burning pain which can grow in intensity and remain with us all day. We rely on strong medications to lessen the pain and most of us have got used to sleepless nights as the new norm. Everything we do is influenced by pain as it controls our minds, thoughts, and activity.

Do we really have to be at the mercy of pain? Why do we allow it to control our lives and thinking? When a child falls over, he cries because he is experiencing pain. He is frightened and looks at the blood falling from the wound and fears the worst. Then mum comes along, gives her child a big hug and reassures him he will be okay. The child then calms down because mum is on the scene and he loves and trusts mum to know best. Her hugs, kisses, washing and dressing the wound have all helped the child to ignore the intensity of his pain. Although the pain is still intense, the child feels much better and doesn't feel the pain as much even though it is still throbbing and very painful.

So how can the child suddenly feel okay with the same amount

Elaine Ballard

of pain? He has been reassured, received love and changed his thinking. His focus is not now so much on the pain but more on his mum as she has taken responsibility for making him better. He feels more secure and relaxes knowing it will be okay because mum has said so.

When I served in the Royal Navy while in Gibraltar, I had a major accident while playing hockey. There were not enough Wrens to form two teams so we played against a tough and very rough male team of sailors. I was hit a few times by sturdy swinging sticks and as a timid goal defender, was deliberately fouled so the ball could enter the net quite freely! At one point, I was in so much pain I could hardly breathe but carried on not wanting to cause a fuss in front of the men or let my team down. After the game, I walked to the netball pitch a few minutes away and began to play goal defense in a netball game. Eventually, I collapsed and was carried off the pitch and taken to hospital. I had crushed two discs and the pain was so severe I couldn't think or talk.

So why didn't I collapse playing hockey? Why didn't I feel the enormity of the pain while still playing? I believe the answer was my determination to continue despite the searing pain. Something else called survival took over. Our minds and thinking play such a vital role in how we react to pain. When pain threatens to overwhelm us, we need to think or be aware of something more important. It may be your children or loved ones who need you. It should be our relationship with our Savior! Like the mom who reassured her son, he no longer concentrated on the pain because he felt secure by his mom's presence. He allowed her to take responsibility for his welfare and his thinking was changed. I carried on playing hockey despite devastating pain because I didn't want to lose face in front of the men. This may have been a foolish decision but the point I am making is, we can control our thinking. The brain controls our body. It sends messages to every part of our body so we can control the pain by the way we think. I am not belittling anyone's pain, mine included. We still may have to take meds to lessen the pain but instead of panicking or worrying, we need to reach out to our Heavenly Father and ask him to take responsibility. We are his beloved children and he will rush to our aid, hold us in his arms, bind our wounds, ease the pain, and reassure us that HE is in control! We need to change our thinking and give him higher priority than the chronic pain.

**PRAYER**

Heavenly Father, thank you that you are always ready to help us in our need. As our Creator and Father, you eagerly run to our aid when we call on you. Your tenderness and healing power is bigger than the pain we have to endure. Help us, Lord, to always believe this. Amen.

## YOU CAN'T BE SERIOUS?

*Always be joyful. Never stop praying. Be thankful in all circumstances, for this is Gods will for you who belong to Christ Jesus. 1Thessalonians 5:16-18 NLT*

I love watching tennis especially seeing top players giving every ounce of their strength to win a tournament. John McEnroe, a former top player, was well known for his remark, "You can't be serious!" He often said this when doubting the umpire's ruling when it didn't go his way. I think as Christians, we are often guilty of talking to God and each other like this. We don't want to make an effort to be joyful or even thankful at the onset of unwanted pain. To be honest I don't even think many of us understand or agree with these verses. But who are we to doubt God's holy word? The New Testament was written by Jesus's disciples who knew him and recorded a great deal of what he said. This scripture should speak to our hearts when we doubt God's wisdom.....

*"All Scripture is inspired by God and is useful to teach us what is true and to make us realize what is wrong in our lives. It corrects us when we are wrong and teaches us to do what is right".*
*2 Timothy 3:16 NLT.*

We must never tell ourselves we cannot praise God when in the middle of a flare. It is possible if we believe that God's word is true. Why is it God's will for us is to praise him in the storm and to thank him? God will never tell us to do anything without a reason. And the reason is always to help us and to glorify himself through us. As we lift our eyes and hearts to the Lord, we are allowing our mind to center upon God who loves us so deeply that he risks our rejection of him. It's hard to let go and allow God to take control of the pain we feel. But as we praise him in song or words, he is lifted up and our hearts are filled with his love and healing. We are obeying him and with obedience comes our reward.

We are not being thankful FOR the pain but thankful because it can bring us closer to the Healer. The closer we are to God, so he can comfort and restore us. He is more likely to ease the pain as well. On a spiritual level we must draw close to our Father to receive from him. On a human level, as we release our praise and worship, our bodies relax more and the tension that pain brings will lesson. The muscles relax releasing pressure on the nerves. So, we can truly be thankful in all circumstances because God in his wisdom has made a way out of the heat of the fiery furnace! We just have to believe this and praise our Lord and Savior while in the middle of the heat.

Have you ever thought by not putting God's precious word into practice; you are throwing his advice back at him? You are telling Almighty God, who knows what is best for you, he is wrong! He has given us precious wise answers to ways of coping when life is tough. It's up to each one of us to take his advice and put it into practice. We either believe his word or we don't!

## PRAYER

Father, forgive us the times we haven't wanted or even believed your word. Your wisdom amazes us. Thank you for your Book of Instructions to guide us in these hard and difficult times. Amen.

## CONTROLLING YOUR PAIN......1

*You made all the delicate, inner parts of my body and knit me together in my mother's womb. Thank you for making me so wonderfully complex! Your workmanship is marvelous — how well I know it. Psalm139:13-14 NLT*

This is my favorite psalm. I often turn to it for comfort when the pain is severe. God reminds me he created every part of my body so he knows exactly what has gone wrong, which part is hurting and why? He is well able to heal me in which way he chooses. That is our problem I think! We want immediate healing. We don't like the pain as it hurts, and chronic pain especially is for life. Our minds cannot adjust easily when pain prevents us from carrying on with our lives as they were. We have grown used to routine and busy lives on the whole. Suddenly we are forced to give up our work and perhaps hobbies we loved doing. We no longer have the same amount of energy to baby sit the grand kids or even our own kids! We feel we are missing out on so much! And then God apparently chooses to let us get on with it because we are not physically healed!

It's understandable that many Christians turn away from God at this point. Some simply stop acknowledging God and forget to read their bibles Praying becomes a nuisance and we no longer have time. Quickly their faith and love for God dwindles and they become cynical. Their faith rests only in what God can do for them rather than in an ever-growing relationship.

To continue in fellowship with our Heavenly Father is essential. He created our bodies and in a way that is beyond our understanding. However, although we can't appreciate what an awesome job he has done, we can allow the Creator to speak to us through his word. Instead of crying and repeating, "It's not fair!" or "Why me?" Stop making the pain the center of our lives. God should be central to every part of our lives. As we focus on him, so he will speak to our hearts.

I believe God has created our minds to control our bodies. Medical people will agree that the brain sends messages to every part. If stress is our reaction, then the brain will pass that on to the whole body. If regret or anger is allowed to reside in our minds, the brain will pass on negative vibes. When our minds are filled with only pain, there is no distraction which the brain can absorb so it centers on pain. I am only too much aware of the level of pain we have. It is more than chronic, it can be acute as well and endless but each one of us has to deal with it. Some days seem impossible to bear but if we have prepared for this cruel pain each day by fellowshipping with our Creator, then it will be automatic to do this on the bad days. Give God time and room to help you relax and feed the brain with good nourishment. The brain will then pass these good foods to the rest of the body. Give credit and praise to our Creator for he made us intricately beautiful and every part for a specific purpose. Don't forget the brain and its power to heal.

## PRAYER

Thank you, Lord, for creating us so perfectly. Forgive us for not wanting to understand the wonderful plan you have for our lives. We confess we have put our own thoughts and desires above your plan and then missed out on your perfect will for us. We praise you for your forgiveness. Amen.

## GIFTS & DISTRACTIONS ...2

*In his grace, God has given us different gifts for doing certain things well. So, if God has given you the ability to prophesy, speak out with as much faith as God has given you. If your gift is serving others, serve them well. If you are a teacher, teach well. If your gift is to encourage others, be encouraging. If it is giving, give generously. If God has given you leadership ability, take the responsibility seriously. And if you have a gift for showing kindness to others, do it gladly. Romans 12:6-8 NLT*

In our last devotion, we were trying to understand how the brain controls our body. The best way to feed the brain with positive nourishment is to spend time every day with God. The bible is filled with words of life and spending time with our Maker praising, learning, and absorbing his presence, our focus is away from the pain.

God tells us in the above verses we have all been given gifts to use. So how do we know what our gift is? Look at the one thing we love doing, are good at, and we see fruit from doing it. It may be your gift is to encourage, to serve in a special way, to pray with people or to pray and intercede for situations. It might be to write poems, letters or even a book. Perhaps it is baking biscuits or cakes for someone. No one can say they have not been given a gift. God's word tells us otherwise. It's simply a matter of thinking about what you enjoy doing.

You may be thinking here of what you used to do and can no longer do it. I was guilty of that too in the beginning. I was born with creative gifts. I loved to make my own clothes, knit long warm winter jumpers, calve animals out of salt blocks, be creative in the garden and pyrography became my every day art. My life changed drastically in 1994 when I was forced to lie in or on my bed all the time. It was devastating and I was very depressed. When I realized my weakened and limited lifestyle I gave up any thought of continuing with any creative gift I might have been given. It was a nightmare come true and I felt redundant, worthless and of no value whatsoever. But as I allowed God in, I found different things I could do while lying down. He was putting suggestions into my heart and a new determination to start again.

I started off with plastic canvas, cutting out shapes and embroidered them with various silks. I made tissue boxes with it for presents. Then I started drawing and painting and learned from a book. Later I wrote two books and many many articles on disability and suffering with the intention of helping other people in a similar situation. I became the Prayer Co-Ordinator for a disability charity. In everything I wrote, it was done lying down using a pencil and paper, then writing it out in pen later. It was physically punishing but God still encouraged me to use the creative gift he had given me from birth. Now I am writing a devotional book on my iPad with one finger. Friends, listen! That gift you have, the desire God has given you, is still there! Yes, you might have to be versatile and rethink how you can still use it but God never recalls his gifts. He expects you to still use it because it was given you for a reason and we will all have to give an account of ourselves one day.

We all need to set our focus away from pain. Our gifts can be distractions because gifts are to be used to help other people. Therefore, it takes the focus off pain and our own discomfort. I know when I am immersed in writing this book or attempting to encourage someone, then I am not so much aware of pain, however bad it is. Of course, there are times when the pain is so intense; we can't physically move to do anything. It's at these times we focus more on Jesus by perhaps listening to music that edifies our soul. Don't give up the gift God has given you. Ask him to show you how to use it in a different way. I know from all I have been through, what I create now bears more fruit than before. Perhaps because it is more costly and God honors this or maybe it's the lessons I have learned through dealing with Arachnoiditis and Adhesive Arachnoiditis as well as CRPS and Allodynia in my legs. They are all experiences I can pass on. God never wastes anything. Your life is still valuable and you can still enjoy life using the amazing gift God chose especially for you!

**PRAYER**
Thank you, Lord, for the good plan you still have for us. Please give us the courage to use our gifts in the way you now intend. Amen.

## GOD'S WORD

*So shall My word be that goes forth from My mouth; It shall not return to Me void, But it shall accomplish what I please, and it shall prosper in the thing for which I sent it. Isaiah 55:11 NKJV*

When I pray I sometimes look up scriptures that relate to my requests. If I am asking for peace I read God's word that talks about peace. I read his many promises and then speak them out aloud. Sometimes I address God's promises to Satan reminding him that God's word will not return void or empty. He cannot stop God's holy word bearing fruit. His word will 'prosper in the thing for which I sent it'. He has spoken and his word is holy. It is God's very breath, nothing can stop it happening. If this is true, why don't we act as if we believe it?

The problem is, while God has given us these promises, he has chosen to hand the responsibility of declaring his word to us, his children. In the beginning God spoke his word and everything was created. But then he gave us authority to look after the world he had made. We are not robots, we have been given the power of choice. It's up to each one of us to choose to read the bible and activate his promises. Sadly, we don't do this enough.

Do we realize the Word is Jesus Christ himself?

*"In the beginning the Word already existed. The Word was with God, and the Word was God. He existed in the beginning with God. God created everything through him, and nothing was created except through him." John 1:1-3 NIV*

The Word (Jesus) already existed in the very beginning and God created everything through Jesus. What an amazing thought! The Father, Son and Holy Spirit were never created, they have always existed.  So, this adds extra significance to God's word. A friend of mine asked me to pray for her. She was taking her driving test the next day and was feeling very nervous having failed the test twice before. Of course, I prayed beforehand but when the actual test was due, I prayed again. This time I bound Satan from using his devious schemes to prevent him from putting obstacles in her way. Then I thanked God for his faithfulness and his promise to direct our paths. The promise of answering our prayers if we keep on asking....was very applicable as this was the third test and so I prayed this verse aloud….

*"Keep on asking, and you will receive what you ask for. Keep on seeking, and you will find. Keep on knocking, and the door will be opened to you." Matthew 7:7 NLT*

Praise God, she passed the test this time!  Trying to cope with Arachnoiditis and its insidious pain and almost impossible challenges, means we need all the help we can get. We need to put on God's full armor to protect our thoughts and minds. We need to appropriate this wonderful gift of God's spoken word. It has power, authority and anointing to reap a harvest of blessings if we will use it.

**PRAYER**

Thank you for your Word, Lord God. Help us to make good choices to speak it out aloud claiming your promises to us. Amen.

## FEAR OR TRUST?

*Don't be afraid, for I am with you. Don't be discouraged, for I am your God. I will strengthen you and help you. I will hold you up with my victorious right hand. Isaiah 41:10*

The bible is full of verses on fear. God knows us very well and understands we will always battle with fear until we come into a living relationship with him through Jesus Christ, his Son. Even as we mature in our walk with him, we will continue to fear but it will grow less and less the more we trust him. Fear and trust are opposites. If we are afraid, we are not trusting God to help us. It's that simple!

Sometimes we think we have overcome or learned a lesson like this. After all, it's so important because if we don't trust God we are putting our trust in our own feelings or abilities to solve a situation. When we have actually trusted God to provide or do something and it happens, we are overjoyed and think we've learned that lesson. But it gets harder the older we become. There are levels of trust and with each situation we face, it becomes more difficult. God wants a deep trust, a trust that says, 'I can't but you can', and to carry on believing his will is very good. It might not look good in our eyes, and we have so many questions, but to trust means we don't need to know the answers and still praise God with a thankful heart.

The last few weeks have been a bit depressing. Something I haven't felt for many years. It hit me hard as I wasn't ready and it shocked me to learn I could still get depressed after all God has taught me and brought me through. It's been tough coming to terms with my legs and feet getting more and more weak and numb from damaged nerves not sending the right signals to my brain. As each day progresses, so my legs slow down to a standstill. By tea time, it's too painful to walk properly and my knees often give way. I knew I needed more personal care. To be truthful I needed more care than my money would allow. In the U.K. Social Care is in crisis and many other disabled or elderly people have to rely on their families or cope alone. I have a small but beautiful apartment with lovely views and have been very happy living here. So, this was a major crisis in my life. My doctor thought the condition of my legs would deteriorate quickly and very soon I would need to go into a Care Home.

So, the journey of fear and trust began. My emotions were tossed about one way, then the other, just like the waves on the sea on a stormy day! My doctor had sent a Village Agent to help me in this process of moving to a Care Home. After she had viewed some local Homes we decided upon one that seemed suitable. My friend helped me clear out my drawers and cupboards and a lot of things went to her home for selling at markets. Another pile was thrown away and yet another pile for auctioning including my furniture. I began to feel sad and wondered if this was right for me. I had no peace because I was not sure what to do. My life was being handled by professionals without me truly knowing it was what God had planned. All the extra mess and work robbed me of more physical strength. I was worn out, tearful and without peace in my heart.

I tried so hard to trust God, knowing this was what I should do. Yet it was the hardest thing of all! It got worse when I discovered Social Services confirmed they would not pay for me to stay in a Care Home when my money ran out in three years' time. In the past, they have usually done this. I suddenly felt very vulnerable for they said I would be moved to a less expensive Care Home or moved into a cheap apartment anywhere in the U.K. We decided to leave the decision for a few days. The forms and brochures of selling my home needed signing and they lay on my bed waiting for my signature. Finally, by God's grace I decided I would trust God in this no matter how I felt. As I made that decision, fear gradually began to dissipate and I asked the Lord to make his will very clear to me. It only took a couple of days for things to become clear and I decided to stay in my apartment for now and trust God to provide all I needed. Amazingly, my legs began to feel stronger almost straight away and I could manage better.

I learned a very valuable lesson. Fear can still catch us at any time. We must be prepared every day to be wearing God's armor to protect our minds especially. If you are fearing the future because of your declining health, stop immediately. Don't carry on harboring fear. It will eat you up inside and peace will disappear. It's a choice we all have to make. To live in fear or trust God completely despite our feelings and circumstances.

**PRAYER**

Lord, help us to trust you no matter what our circumstances are like. Give us grace to acknowledge you always know best when we feel weak and fearful, and trust you completely. Amen.

## ANGER

*Get rid of all bitterness, rage, anger, harsh words and slander, as well*
*as all types of evil behavior. Instead, be kind to each other,*
*tenderhearted, forgiving one another, just as God through*
*Christ has forgiven you. Ephesians 4:31-32 NLT*

Anger is a very common problem these days. I think in general
most people are very busy and in more of a hurry. With social
media being more prominent everything is more instantaneous.
As a society, we have perhaps become very impatient. It's easy
to be irritated and if this is not checked, anger takes over and
can become a filter through which we see and deal with
everything else.

I think we all understand when we are uptight and frustrated;
these emotions can affect our bodies. Our muscles tighten
affecting the damaged nerves and we cannot think as clearly as
we should. A healthy person is more able to cope with anger
and frustration but for us who are struggling with a
neurological disease such as Arachnoiditis, it is even more
difficult. Chronic pain that never goes away is hard to deal
with. Our brains are constantly tired from having to work
through the fog of severe and constant pain and our thinking
ability is impaired. Blood pressure can also rise, affecting the
heart. So how can we stop anger and frustration taking over?

Jesus himself experienced anger....

*"Jesus made a whip from some ropes and chased them all out of the Temple. He drove out the sheep and cattle, scattered the money changers' coins over the floor, and turned over their tables. Then, going over to the people who sold doves, he told them, "Get these things out of here. Stop turning my Father's house into a marketplace!" Then his disciples remembered this prophecy from the Scriptures: "Passion for God's house will consume me.""*
*John 2:15-17 NLT*

I do believe Jesus understands our feelings and emotions. He was fully human as well as Divine and felt anger. But his anger was a righteous anger which he dealt with and then carried on with his ministry. We can tell ourselves the anger we feel is righteous as the situations against us are unfair. We want justice if a medical professional has caused us harm. I understand, but I also understand if we hold on to anger whether it be targeted at a doctor or this disease, it will harm us physically and mentally.

As Christians, we know it is important to forgive. Forgiveness does not mean we have to accept a wrong or indeed stay in contact with someone. God gives us a good reason why we should forgive.

*"But if you refuse to forgive others, your Father will not forgive your sins." Matthew 6:15 NLT*

We must take this warning very seriously. Sometimes we think if we forgive someone or blaming an illness in anger, we are letting them get away with their wrong doing. Vengeance and retribution belongs to God, not us. Anger will always eat away inside us causing more pain than before. Make a decision to hand the anger over to Almighty God. He is well able to deal with that person or your feelings towards the disease that has offended you.

**PRAYER**

Father, we ask forgiveness for any anger we have allowed to stay inside us. Cleanse our hearts, minds, and spirits so you can use us more for your Kingdom. Amen.

## FEELING GUILTY?

*I eagerly expect and hope that I will in no way be ashamed, but will have sufficient courage so that now as always Christ will be exalted in my body, whether by life or by death. Philippians 1:20 NIV*

When I first had the word 'disabled' attached to me in 1994, I felt a little ashamed. The world of disability still had a stigma attached to it and family and some friends struggled with their embarrassment of not knowing what to say. After a year of lying in and on the bed upstairs, we managed to get funds to help with buying a stair lift. A whole new world suddenly opened up to me. No longer was I confined to my upstairs bedroom. Determined to get out in my wheelchair and enjoy the breath of fresh air caressing my face was wonderful. The smallest things seemed so important and helped make me feel more normal.

However, I soon discovered many problems. It didn't matter who was pushing the wheelchair, whenever we stopped to say hello to a passing neighbor, the wheelchair was not turned around so I could have face to face contact. I was left out of conversations and this increased my sense of guilt. I was different and would always be treated this way. I tried accessing several facilities put on for people with disabilities. Each time I was refused because my fold up bed was considered a fire hazard. I could sit but only for about five minutes. So, the idea of taking a fold up bed to church and social functions for disabled people felt a good idea.

Going to church with my bed worked okay but it took all six deacons to sit around my bed discussing the pros and cons of my bed being in their church. Most deacons were fine about it but two felt if I was able to do this, then they couldn't refuse other people. However, eventually it was agreed.

At first my experience was positive as children were naturally inquisitive to explore the bed and my new electric wheelchair. Their eagerness and sense of wanting to look after me helped me relax. But later on, I found I was becoming the subject of visiting speakers' sermons. I was often used as an example of what they wanted to say. One Sunday a young aspiring healer approached me after the service and began praying. The canvas bed swayed as his legs came into contact with the thin material I lay on. He shook as he 'felt' the anointing of God's Spirit and prophesied healing over me. He was young but the experience made me realize I would never be accepted for who I was. It took two years before I could open my heart for the Lord to heal me. The guilt had embedded itself inside but healing did come and I am so thankful to God for it.

It takes courage to accept ourselves as we are. Some people reject us through misunderstanding Arachnoiditis. Others are embarrassed and don't know what to say. It's a difficult disease for our friends to accept because they can't identify with it. In his word, God tells us to take courage and believe Christ can still be exalted in our new pain torn bodies. In fact, he is able to use us more because of what we have experienced. Never accept negative things people put onto us. We are children of the Most-High God! Loved and forgiven! Accepted because of the sacrifice made at the Cross on our behalf. We have nothing to feel guilty about. God knows what has happened to us and he has allowed this disease to come into our lives. Remember, if you are totally surrendered to God, he will bring good out of this:

*"And we know that God causes everything to work together for the good of those who love God and are called according to his purpose for them. Romans 8:28 NLT*

In fact, the 'good' can be 'great' if we embrace what God has allowed. The difference between accepting and embracing means we put all that we have into the new life without complaint and allow God to work out his will in us. And our life will have a new purpose and God says it will be GOOD!

**PRAYER**
Thank you, Father, we are accepted just as we are through Jesus' sacrifice on the Cross. We let go of the guilt and shame and receive your total acceptance and deep cleansing love. Amen.

## ALONE OR LONELY?

*Then Jesus said, "Let's go off by ourselves to a quiet place and rest awhile." He said this because there were so many people coming and going that Jesus and his apostles didn't even have time to eat.*
*Mark 6:31 NLT*

I have experienced both alone and lonely times in my life. They are very different. In the above scripture Jesus and his disciples had been very busy as so many people kept being drawn to Jesus and were curious to see and hear what he had to say. Even Jesus must have felt very tired at times. There are always people in family life who demand our attention and this constant pressure adds more pain. Sometimes we go beyond our ability to help people feel comfortable around us. I know my brain feels extremely tired after a visit. Even talking drains my energy so quickly. I can't seem to think clearly and my brain tends to shut down without notice. But it's not just the brain that gets tired. Lying down on my side, talking and listening, always causes a great deal of pain. Without realizing, I lift my head slightly to see the person better and the angle is never right. So, I tend to have to either raise my head on the pillow or lower it to be in a more comfortable position to see the visitor more clearly. It only takes a minute adjustment of my head and it causes acute pain later.

We all need time to ourselves to recover from being busy. Pain is strange how it saps our energy and leaves us feeling weak and exhausted. If Jesus needed time alone from the crowds, then we surely do as well. On many occasions, the bible tells us

Jesus withdrew from his disciples to be alone with his Father and pray.

These times with our Heavenly Father are precious and essential. We need to keep up our daily quiet time and spend quality time reading his word, in worship and prayer. Nothing can replace this special time because it fills us with peace as we are in the presence of God. How do we get to know friends better? We hang out with them, talking, and listening to each other. Our friendship grows in this way. And so, it is the same with our beloved Lord.

Loneliness is very different. As a child, I always felt lonely as I was too shy to take the initiative to talk to people. It was too costly to risk being rejected. Happy to say the Lord gradually changed me into a more outgoing person who loved people so much, the fear of rejection faded away. But I still remember clearly the times at school when no one played with me and I hid from boys in case I had to speak to them. I often felt lonely in company, a strange thing to experience as I needed friends so badly.

This disease can cause us to feel we are completely by ourselves especially if living on our own. It's so important to try and keep in contact with friends or make new ones. I have on two occasions made enquiries about local churches to see if they have a visiting ministry. Some churches do have people who will visit and even bring communion to your home if you cannot get to a church. There are charities, too, who offer telephone conversations or have an active visiting ministry. I have found this invaluable and have a phone friend who rings me at a certain time and day each week. We have sent each other photos of ourselves and photos of our hobbies. Loneliness can lead to depression if we are not careful, and let's face it, with all we have to cope with each day; it's good to have someone to share with. I had never been a member of a support group until I was diagnosed with Arachnoiditis and felt so bewildered by the name and what it might do to my body. Joining a support group was the best thing I did for they had so many files to read about this disease, as well as meeting a wonderful group of people all trying to support each other. I do encourage anyone who has been diagnosed with any difficult condition or disease to find a good support group. We all need people in our lives who will encourage us and know exactly what we are going through.

**PRAYER**
Thank you, Lord, for the people you bring to us. They are handpicked by you for nothing in your Kingdom happens by chance. We praise you, too, for those precious moments in your presence where we are drawn closer. Thank you for your unending love and mercy. Amen.

## GOD IS FAITHFUL

*The faithful love of the Lord never ends! His mercies never cease. Great is his faithfulness; his mercies begin afresh each morning. I therefore, I will hope in him! Lamentations 3:22-24 NLT*

What are we hoping for? Where have we put our trust? The answer is found in believing in the faithfulness of God. We cannot have hope for the future unless we sincerely believe that God is faithful. At the beginning of the above verses we are reminded that God's is faithful in loving us. The word faithful means to be trusted, constant, true, loyal and unchanging. What more could we ask our Heavenly Father to be? His faithful love also never ends. It continues on and on, forever. Of course, we don't want to sin thinking it doesn't matter as God will always love us.  No, if we did that I am sure God would punish us for disobeying him. Parents discipline their children for wrong doing so they learn to do what is right. So, our Heavenly Father disciplines us because he wants the best for us.

Another reason to believe in God's faithfulness is, *'his mercies never cease ....his mercies begin afresh each morning'. (Lamentations 3:22-23).* He not only loves us deeply and faithfully but each day is a fresh beginning. Do you ever have a day when you mess up first thing and you feel sorry and wonder how you ever got into that particular mess? It might be something you said or had a wrong attitude but it happened and you just want to start the day again with a blank check. The amazing thing is, we all can! Every morning is a new day and yesterday has been wiped clean. If we are sorry then God forgives us and we start again.

All of us should have hope while we are on this journey on earth. But even if life continues to be very hard God promises to bring good from it. And from experience I can say I have known a deeper joy as a result of refining at the hands of the Great Potter.

*"The Lord is my inheritance; therefore I will hope in him."*
*Lamentations 3:24 NIV*

This last part of our scripture today speaks of putting our hope in God. It's good to have hope but it is also important to trust that where we are placing our hope is totally secure. As children of God we should feel secure in our inheritance. Whatever is part of God's Kingdom will be ours too. We have inherited some already. The Name of Jesus Christ, the work of the Holy Spirit within us, the power of the blood of Christ, healing in the blood of Christ, resurrection from the dead, God's eternal word, joy, peace, righteousness and much more. So once we have tasted some of our inheritance we know we can rest in our faithful God to keep his promises to us. He will continue faithfully loving us right through to the very end of our time here on earth and into Heaven where we will spend eternity with him! Hallelujah!

**PRAYER**
Thank you, Lord, for the wonderful inheritance you have given us. We praise you for not keeping a record of our sins. Each day is a new beginning, how amazing! Great and secure is your faithfulness O Lord! Amen.

## WHY PRAY?

*I looked for someone among them who would build up the wall and stand before me in the gap on behalf of the land so I would not have to destroy it, but I found no one.  Ezekiel 22:30 NIV*

Many Christians believe in prayer but do not see it as the most important thing they can do. They do not see prayer as a ministry. Perhaps they give God a few minutes and read their bible each day and then wonder why they don't see the answers. Prayer meetings at most churches have the lowest attendance whereas Sunday services, bible studies and social activities seem more attractive.

We have many opportunities to pray for each other if we belong to a support group or have a Facebook page. Living with Arachnoiditis is extremely hard as we have so many challenges and chronic pain to cope with. It's a disease that often progresses and if we don't ask for prayer support we are missing out on something very powerful. When we see someone asking for prayer as they describe the bad day they are having, how do we respond? Do we say, yes I will pray, then take it to the Lord and leave it? Or do we pray every day for a while and then ask them how they are? Real caring is just this. One quick prayer is not what we need. We need our hearts aligned with this person's needs and pray each day. It can mean a great deal more when someone gets in touch to say they have been praying and followed through.

It takes time and a willingness to learn and truly care about people to understand how we should pray, and to pray effectively. I felt a call to a life of prayer very soon after becoming a Christian. I didn't think God wanted me to live in a convent or shut myself away from people but I knew praying was to be a big part of my life. As I tried to put it into practice, I told my minister and asked how I could pray for him? He took my calling seriously and shared a few things to pray for. I felt so excited as I sat down and prayed. After ten minutes though I ran out of words. I had no idea that prayer had more depth than this.

Over the years God has taught me a deeper side to praying. Use the bible as it's full of God's promises. Repeat the promise aloud and claim it for the person for whom you are praying. Or indeed for your own situation. The enemy is listening and trembles at God's inspired word. This is very powerful as we can bind Satan with the word of God and using the wonderful Name of Jesus Christ! We can pray in the Spirit, knowing he intercedes for us. I often ask the Holy Spirit to intercede especially when I have prayed and feel my prayers have not been sufficient. We need to remember prayer is a spiritual battle and our enemy is the devil who wants to stop our prayers reaching God's heart.

*"We do not know what we ought to pray for, but the Spirit himself intercedes for us through wordless groans. And he who searches our hearts knows the mind of the Spirit, because the Spirit intercedes for God's people in accordance with the will of God."*
*Romans 8:26-27 NIV.*

Yes, prayer is a battle! We should know God's love deep within our hearts. As soon as we know someone is asking for help, then start praying God's word over them. His word will never return to him without producing fruit. On occasions, I have actually felt a warmth and peace which assured me that people were praying. Praying for another Arachnoiditis sufferer can open the way for our Lord to use you in this special ministry. You understand all too well what a bad day means. You can now empathize, as you are able to feel their pain, so let's keep on interceding, lifting our brothers and sisters up in a real and caring way. Let's fight this battle together!

**PRAYER**

Thank you, Lord, for showing us how to pray. Fill our hearts with your deep caring love so we can share in the pain of others. Amen.

## JOY IS NOT LACK OF TROUBLE

*Our hearts ache, but we always have joy. We are poor, but we give spiritual riches to others. We own nothing, and yet we have everything.  2 Corinthians 6:10 NLT*

What makes us happy? We might answer, being 'in love', meeting the person of our dreams or good friends and family. Perhaps happiness comes from eating at our favorite restaurant or having new clothes. I used to love dancing and playing netball. I loved anything creative.....art, crocheting, cross stitch, pyrography or perhaps playing games on my iPad! Of course, there is a certain amount of happiness we can have from these things but it is only temporary. Relationships can and often do go wrong causing stress, bad feeling, and disappointment. If we put all our hope in our business bringing us happiness, we have forgotten the times when we had financial difficulties, or employees let us down. Perhaps there were sacrifices we made in order to make our business a success.

Arachnoiditis costs a great deal. We all had a life before and now we are thinking of what we lost. Chronic pain limits us enormously as we try and carry on living the way we used to. There comes a time when we have to admit we have to do less. Unfortunately, at this time, many of us get depressed as life can never be the same and we grieve over our loss. Happiness goes out the window and it's never replaced.

We need to understand that happiness in only temporary and it's not the 'things' we do that will give us joy. Lasting happiness

can only come through a personal relationship with God
through Jesus Christ. We need to discover the joy that comes
from knowing Christ and embrace it. It will bring us more
happiness than a temporary and fragile emotion. Paul wrote,

*"You have greatly encouraged me and made me happy despite all our
troubles." 2 Corinthians 7:4 NLT*

Real happiness that comes from a deep embedded joy, does not
depend on our circumstances. Good health doesn't necessarily
make us happy either.

I think we need to refocus our thoughts and ideas about what is
of true and lasting value. It is easy to center on the world's ideas
of what makes them happy. The things that will last and bring
us deep inner joys are peace, forgiveness, Christ centered love,
and purpose in life. These can only be found in knowing God
through Jesus Christ. As we surrender our lives to God so he
changes our thought patterns and priorities. What is real and
what is not. To have a thorn in our flesh means God will use the
thorn to refine us. He always uses everything that is given to
him. Our focus then is not on regret or loss, but we focus on
God, get to know him more and wait for him as he prepares us
for a new adventure. Life can still be exciting and filled with
meaning and purpose too.

## PRAYER

Lord God, forgive us for focusing on our loss and regret. We hand everything to you. Please take full control and prepare us for whatever is ahead. We believe what has happened will turn out for our good and bring you great glory! Amen.

## GOD'S GRACE

*Three different times I begged the Lord to take it away. Each time he said, "My grace is all you need. My power works best in weakness." So now I am glad to boast about my weaknesses, so that the power of Christ can work through me.* *2 Corinthians 12:8-9 NLT*

Paul refers in this scripture to a thorn in his flesh. No one knows exactly what the 'thorn' was and bible scholars have made many suggestions. Perhaps it's good we don't know because it means all of us can identify with Paul's frustrations. He finds this thorn a tremendous struggle and begs the Lord to remove it. Sound familiar? God responds to Paul's prayers by saying, "My grace is all you need". His answer reveals so much for God's grace can only be given to his children. People who have refused his love and invitation to give their lives to him, have deliberately turned their backs on God and therefore on his gifts. Receiving God's grace is the only way we can understand and live life in a richer way than before.

Understanding the Lord's grace is key to applying it to our lives. We don't want to live with Arachnoiditis through acceptance. This comes from ourselves, a decision we made out of desperation. The answer to a good life with purpose can only come in a supernatural way. Trying to live with such a debilitating and painful disease made us aware of our own weakness and severe limitations. We tried everything possible to get better. Different medicines, different doctors, different ways of doing things, but all we discovered was our own humanity. We are weaker physically, mentally and emotionally and we need something far bigger than us to make a difference in our lives. God's answer is to pour out his grace upon us when he doesn't take the problem away. When at last we understand that God's grace is able to change us, make us strong and gives us wisdom in our situation, then we can stop trying to cope in our own limited resources.

Joseph was disowned and badly treated by his brothers. He was thrown into prison and stayed there for many years. But he didn't question God but simply carried on living this new difficult life as a witness to God's faithfulness. He looked to God, prayed and God gave him favor and wisdom which came through his grace. It is not just a word without meaning. Grace contains all the gifts and mercy and love of God.

*"And God gave him favor before Pharaoh, king of Egypt. God also gave Joseph unusual wisdom, so that Pharaoh appointed him governor over all of Egypt and put him in charge of the palace."*
*Acts of the Apostles 7:9-10 NLT*

God gave Joseph all the gifts and resources he needed for his situation. He can do the same for us if we ask. Stop looking at our own limitations and start receiving and living in the grace of God because it really is quite amazing!

We have to retrain our minds to see our lives from God's perspective which is totally opposite from ours. "My power works best in weakness" is quite a statement! But if we look back to the time we accepted Jesus Christ, it's clear we understood that Jesus Christ was Lord. If Lord, then we recognized our own weakness and need of a stronger power in our lives. So, every time we find ourselves facing a very difficult situation, we should cry out to God for his grace because we recognize God is able to give us the strength and power we need.

**PRAYER**

How self-centered can we be Lord? Please forgive us for refusing to believe your grace holds everything we need to live a victorious life. Amen.

## WHERE IS PEACE?

*I have told you all this so that you may have peace in me. Here on earth you will have many trials and sorrows. But take heart, because I have overcome the world.  John 16:33 NLT*

We have so much in our day to day lives that can take away our peace. When our bodies are aggressively raging in pain or we constantly think about the future and what might happen, peace cannot be found! We become what we are thinking about and then we can't stop ourselves from being a little bad tempered. To change our mind set takes practice and determination but it can be done.

These days I sometimes have to deal with pain that refuses to lessen in my legs, weakness, and rapidly increasing numbness. I have been diagnosed with Allodynia. Every day, towards late afternoon, I know my legs will not move well. It's here I have a choice to make. Do I give in to negativity and focus on the 'what if's', or do I commit it all to the Lord?

We may not understand why we have to go through certain things; all I know is we live in a fallen world. God created a perfect world where pain and conflict did not exist but when he created human beings, he gave us power....power to choose how to react. Sin and disease entered the world with Adam and Eve. It was their choice to disobey God and eat an apple which was forbidden. So, generations later, God still gives us the same choice. We know what we should do and how we should behave but we count it too hard to bother. Is our Lord's sacrifice wasted? Is it simply a nice story or can we make the right choice to appropriate the victory of the Cross to our own lives? Jesus gave up everything so we might live in peace but that means obedience and worship in the middle of the flames. Don't live by how you feel but change your mind set so you focus on his word and upon God himself.

God has not brought disease and sickness upon us, he loves us, but he does expect us to surrender everything to him. As we do, he will pour his strength into our ailing bodies and fill us with his peace as we trust him to help and use us. The Christian's life is about reflecting the glory of God to everyone around. The more difficult our journey, the deeper the reflection of God may be seen in us. It's a privileged life but not many will take up the challenge. The choice is ours. What will you choose today?

**PRAYER**
Lord, there are so many things to take away our peace. Help us to keep our hearts and minds on you for you have won the victory for us. All we need to do is trust completely in your sovereignty over our situations. Thank you gracious Lord! Amen.

## GOD NEW BEFORE YOU DID

*But everything they did was determined beforehand according to your will.  Acts of the Apostles 4:28 NLT*

The disciples had lost their Teacher, Lord and Master and great Friend. They were frightened they would be arrested and tortured just as Jesus was. The agony and horror of the crucifixion must have weighed heavily upon them as they finally saw Jesus dead and placed in a tomb. We can imagine how frightened they were. But they didn't allow their feelings to dictate what they did. The Lord had revealed himself to them after the resurrection so they knew he had risen from the dead. They even started to preach the good news to the people and heal them. However, opposition from the authorities rose up but they were determined to praise God as they met together. Their prayer was to ask for boldness to carry on preaching and the day came when God answered their prayers.

*"On the day of Pentecost all the believers were meeting together in one place. Suddenly, there was a sound from heaven like the roaring of a mighty windstorm, and it filled the house where they were sitting." Acts of the Apostles 2:1-2 NLT*

I can imagine as the disciples remembered the trial before Pilate and consequent scourging, crucifixion and the resurrection, they were able to understand that God had planned all that took place. Jesus was not taken by force and crucified against his will. He knew the scriptures that spoke of his Father's plan for salvation. He knew he was the Sacrificial Lamb who would carry all our sin so we could live in freedom and victory.

It's so reassuring to know God has determined the circumstances of our lives before they ever happened. As he poured out his strength and healing power to his disciples, so he will do the same for us. God knows all the difficulties of the past, present and those ahead and he already has provided the answers. So, don't give up! Believe what his word is telling us that God already knew this disease would attack our bodies. Look up and listen for his answers because our Lord would not leave us in such a mess without having planned solutions for our good. Get together with other Christians and pray, just like the disciples, with boldness and great expectation that God's preplanned will, will be done. Pray with great faith and expect miracles to happen! God knew the problem before you did; trust him to have the answers!

**PRAYER**

How amazing it is, Lord God that our lives have been planned out by you. Forgive us when we only look at the problems. We ask you to help us seek your good plan in everything we face. Amen.

*Elaine Ballard*

## REASONS TO FORGIVE....1

*Do not judge others, and you will not be judged. For you will be treated as you treat others. The standard you use in judging is the standard by which you will be judged. Matthew 7:1-2 NLT*

There is a great deal of misunderstanding about forgiveness. We know the bible tells us to forgive everyone who has hurt or offended us but it isn't easy. Friends leave us when they discover we can't go out socially anymore. Doctors have lied or refused to help. Family sometimes don't want to read the files we give them to help understand Arachnoiditis. Life seems unfair. Trying to get financial support may leave us depressed. We get hurt, upset, depressed, and God expects us to forgive. How is this possible?

There are many scriptures to help us…

*"..be kind to each other, tenderhearted, forgiving one another, just as God through Christ has forgiven you." Ephesians 4:32 NLT*

Here we are told to forgive because God has forgiven us. That's true; we have all offended God by our lack of commitment and certainly not trusting him when life has become very difficult. We cry out for healing but if he chooses not to, some of us refuse to believe he has a greater or different plan. We dig our spiritual heals in and think our own understanding is far superior than God's plan.

These next two scriptures are hard to accept, nevertheless they have been written by Christ's disciples for our benefit. Our Lord taught his disciples…

*"Forgive others, and you will be forgiven." Luke 6:37 NLT*

*"There will be no mercy for those who have not shown mercy to others. But if you have been merciful, God will be merciful when he judges you." James 2:13 NLT.*

God is telling us unless we forgive, he will not forgive us! Quite a thought isn't it? We need to understand that God wants us to have pure hearts so he can use us more. His message of unconditional love and forgiveness cannot be effective through a filter of bitterness. He wants to get our attention and this teaching certainly does that.

But then the Lord goes a step further and says we must not even remember their sin.

*"For I will be merciful to their unrighteousness, and their sins and their lawless deeds I will remember no more" Hebrews 8:12 NKJV*

Now this is what I call forgiveness at its best. I believe it's impossible to forgive extreme wrong doing in our own strength. It plays in our minds over and over and we haven't the resources to do this. That's where God's grace takes over as we have talked about before. If we truly want to forgive and forget we must take it to the Lord and ask for the gift of his grace. We need God's power to help us and we mustn't under estimate the power there is in grace. All of God's attributes and abilities are wrapped up in this amazing gift. We have to deny our feelings that want justice and 'put on' the grace of God. If he can forgive and forget our sin, then we can do the same.

Forgiveness may not happen all at once and we must allow ourselves a little time until we are in a position of grace and able to forgive. However, it is also a choice and we must make that decision even when our feelings need to catch up. Forgiving means we release them from their offense. We no longer want retribution; in fact we pray God's blessings upon them. We are not condoning what they have done and neither are we saying we will be best buddies either. No, forgiving someone means acknowledging the wrong but being wise as well. If they are not contrite it's impossible to continue the relationship or still see the same doctor. Forgiveness acknowledges the sin but chooses to forget by refusing to talk about it or replaying it in the mind. It isn't easy but Christ forgave us and forgets our sins. The reason for this teaching is God created us for fellowship with himself and to use us to spread the message of his love which will bring glory to himself. We must be pure and holy. We cannot say, well, I have forgiven the doctor or nurse or friend and say we hate the disease! Wrong! Almighty God has allowed this disease in our lives so we cannot tell him his plan is awful! We must accept and embrace this new plan and seek God, asking him to reveal our part in it. We are still priceless, worthwhile, made beautiful and forgiven in Christ Jesus. Ask God how he wants to use you and he will answer in ways that might astound you.

**PRAYER**

Help us, Father, to forgive as you forgave. We are sorry to have held on to bitterness and anger. Please reveal your perfect will for us in this painful disease. We trust your plans for our lives. Amen.

## FORGIVING YOURSELF ....2

*I am Joseph, your brother, whom you sold into slavery in Egypt. But don't be upset, and don't be angry with yourselves for selling me to this place. It was God who sent me here ahead of you to preserve your lives. Genesis 45:4-5 NLT*

I love reading about the story of Joseph. It's a great story of love triumphing over hate, forgiveness over sin, God's faithfulness to his promises, and victory over tragedy. Joseph was the youngest half-brother of a large family and was given the job of looking after his father's sheep. His brothers despised him because Joseph was their father's favorite and they were jealous. Joseph also reported back to his father every time his brothers were doing something wrong. Then their father gave Joseph a beautiful coat of many colors as he was born to him in his old age. Joseph had a couple of dreams and in one he sees all his brothers bowing down to him and God tells Joseph he will make him king one day. Joseph had a lot to learn and instead of keeping these dreams to himself, he told his brothers causing them to hate him even more. One day they captured Joseph and put him in a cistern and sold him into slavery and eventually prison where he suffered a great deal. His life changed dramatically but Joseph was in the place God had planned all along for it was in these years Joseph learned the ways of God. He was being prepared for his role as the king's right hand man and saved his country from devastating famine.

I expect Joseph had plenty of time in prison while God worked in his life and helped him to forgive his brothers and forgive himself too. His brothers were guilty for how they treated him but Joseph was guilty too for his attitude and feeding their jealousy. Our scripture today explains it was very important to Joseph that his brothers forgive themselves. "Don't be upset, and don't be angry with yourselves..." He can see God's hand in it all. "It was God who sent me here ahead of you to preserve your lives."

We can see clearly that God has a purpose and plan for everyone. But first of all, we have to forgive ourselves so we can forgive someone else. It's much harder to forgive if we are harboring guilt or anger inside. God knows this and draws us into this great story. As we forgive ourselves we release everything that is toxic and we can know total freedom inside.

Many Christians live with guilt and fear which will, in time, consume them. Regret over words we have spoken or actions taken will cause us to feel guilty. This is one reason why we should keep short accounts with God. If we bury the guilt it will slowly eat away and find its ugly head in different aspects of our life. Fear comes when we think we don't deserve to be forgiven or the person we have offended refuses to forgive us. Forgiving ourselves shouldn't depend on the other person's response. We need to own our responsibilities and not look to others to live our lives. Fear is a very toxic emotion as it is opposite to love.

*"There is no fear in love. But perfect love drives out fear, because fear has to do with punishment. The one who fears is not made perfect in love." 1 John 4:18 NIV*

We cannot love properly while filled with fear. Feeling we should be punished is telling Jesus his sacrifice was in vain. All our sin has been dealt with at the Cross, through the sufferings of Christ. We must not throw it back at him by holding on to the guilt and fear of what we have done. Jesus was punished for our sin. Fear and guilt has been dealt with once and for all! There is no other punishment, isn't that wonderful? Relax, forgive others, forgive yourself and live in freedom. And remember, just as God caused everything to work together for good in Joseph's life, so he is already doing that for you and me.

*"And we know that God causes everything to work together for the good of those who love God and are called according to his purpose for them." Romans 8:28 NLT*

**PRAYER**
Lord God, thank you for helping us understand why we should forgive ourselves. We offer up all the fear and guilt for you have already paid the sacrifice for our sins. There is no more fear of punishment. The price has been paid, hallelujah!  Amen.

## IS SUICIDE A WAY OUT?

*I can never escape from your Spirit! I can never get away from your presence! If I go up to heaven, you are there; if I go down to the grave, you are there.....I could ask the darkness to hide me and the light around me to become night— but even in darkness I cannot hide from you. To you the night shines as bright as day. Darkness and light are the same to you. Psalms 139:7-8, 11-12 NLT*

I know there are many who suffer continuously with chronic and acute pain who reach a point of no return. When the pain is overwhelming and carries on day and night after night, reality is put on hold as we try and face each day. Tiredness leads to exhaustion as sleep refuses to come and even light sleep evades us. Some writers have a problem writing on a certain subject because although they may be excellent writers, they haven't actually experienced what they want to write about. However, I do feel well qualified to write on this particular subject. I have battled with multi-level disc disease for 50 years after a sporting accident and believe the last 23 years I have had Arachnoiditis as well. I was not aware of support groups before I had my iPad so most of those years I have had to soldier on without any doctor's support or understanding from friends and family. It was so difficult keeping going on my own that I pushed down any negative thoughts and pretended I was fine. Eventually, depression set in and thoughts of suicide were my constant companion.

When we are so low reality disappears and responsibility for our actions is sometimes blurry. Our minds and thinking are changed as we try so desperately to hang in. Many years ago, took an overdose of tablets on two separate occasions. My mind was confused as I didn't want to die but saw no other way out. I desperately needed help, any help, medical or simply someone to understand and not whisper about me when they thought I couldn't hear. They were cries for help! I knew I might die as I swallowed sufficient for that to happen. Before each time I prayed asking for forgiveness but begged God to send me human help. I say human help because during those very dark times, I felt God was not sufficient. I needed a human being to tell me they loved and understood all I was going through. I think I did want to die but was scared if I did, I was risking my salvation! I did truly love Jesus and my life was totally committed to him. But I couldn't carry on without human help. I felt God was simply not enough!!

I think it's very important to face this subject as more and more Arachnoiditis sufferers are finding no other way than to commit suicide. So, let's think a little about what happens when we reach this point of no return and hopefully shed some light and encouragement to prevent it happening.

What is exactly happening to us as we think about suicide? What are we looking for? I believe Satan is attacking our minds but we don't recognize it as an attack. He represents darkness and will do his best to fill our minds with his lies. He is God's greatest enemy and will attack God's children at every opportunity. He surrounds us in his own darkness, draws us in to believe all hope has gone and death is the only option. We have become so desperate for relief from this insidious cruel pain, we see no other option. But is this true? Satan is the father of all lies so we must remember at these times never to believe these thoughts. Prepare our minds even now so we are not deceived later on.

The truth is, we can never get away from these burdens we carry. Satan cannot release us from them and death will not free us either. If we die we have not escaped because God is everywhere and we will have to give an account for our actions. Our scripture for today tells us that we can never escape from his Spirit. God's presence is everywhere. We cannot hide in the darkness for God is Light and his Light consumes the darkness. There is no way we can escape God for he is literally everywhere. Why would we want to escape God anyway? The shame and guilt of suicide will haunt us for although it is understandable, it is wrong and goes against God's law of committing murder on ourselves. He created us and we belong to him.

However, God does understand our humanity and I have no doubt he will show compassion and love to us. But can we risk our salvation? We can't be absolutely sure. However, the bible does tell us nothing can separate us from his love.

*"And I am convinced that nothing can ever separate us from God's love. Neither death nor life, neither angels nor demons, neither our fears for today nor our worries about tomorrow—not even the powers of hell can separate us from God's love." Romans 8:38 NLT*

These are comforting words and yet we have to consider as

well, if we committed suicide, would we lose our rewards in heaven? Yes, we might still keep our salvation but I am looking forward to all those rewards God wants to lavish on me for the times I overcame and didn't give up.

*"And remember that the heavenly Father to whom you pray has no favorites. He will judge or reward you according to what you do. So you must live in reverent fear of him during your time here as "temporary residents.""* 1 Peter 1:17 NLT

God loves us and understands every pain and doubt we have. He sent his beloved Son, Jesus Christ, to earth to die in our place and bear all our sins. His death is sufficient to free us from the agonies of this life on earth. We need to hang in when we are tempted and command the enemy to leave us alone in Jesus' Name. Talk to someone and talk to Jesus who understands all we go through. One day God will bring justice for all we are suffering and we will be overjoyed we hung in and believed God would make it right.

*"For I, the Lord, love justice. I hate robbery and wrongdoing. I will faithfully reward my people for their suffering and make an everlasting covenant with them."* Isaiah 61:8 NLT

Those rewards are waiting for us now. Hang in, for this life is temporary and it will soon be over and we will then stand before our loving Savior and God and rejoice together that we did indeed overcome!! This can happen now and not wait until we go to heaven because God is a miracle worker and can do all these things. Trust him in these dark moments to make his promises come true for he is not a man that he should lie....

*"God is not a man, so he does not lie. He is not human, so he does not change his mind. Has he ever spoken and failed to act? Has he ever promised and not carried it through?"* Numbers 23:19 NLT

**PRAYER**
Sovereign Lord, we know you understand our weaknesses because you overcame your own temptations here on earth. Help us, Lord, in these dire moments to reach out to you and not give in. Amen.

## THE CROWN OF LIFE

*Blessed is the one who perseveres under trial because, having stood the test, that person will receive the crown of life that the Lord has promised to those who love him. James 1:12 NIV*

I have had multi-level disc disease for 50 years which began with a sporting accident, and I believe for the last 23 years, I have lived with Arachnoiditis and Adhesive Arachnoiditis but only diagnosed 2 years ago. It's been quite a journey! I have struggled and squirmed, shed many tears but also learned more about myself and the immeasurable grace and love of God. I have been taught in the College of Life by the greatest Teacher of all time, Jesus Christ and his colleague, The Holy Spirit. There have been many lessons to learn but the one I am most grateful for is the lesson of perseverance. It has seen me through many times when I felt like giving up, but didn't, because I wanted to pass this particular exam for it is the glue that holds everything together. Without knowing how to persevere, I would have failed all the other exams. It's that important! Unfortunately, it takes years of hard work and sadly I had to redo this exam many times.

So, what is perseverance and how do we pass this exam? Life is full of learning and taking tests. First of all, God wants us to be different from the world....

*"But you are a chosen people, a royal priesthood, a holy nation, God's special possession, that you may declare the praises of him who called you out of darkness into his wonderful light." 1 Peter 2:9 NIV*

As Christians we have been hand-picked, chosen by God to be his Bride, and to declare the message of salvation to people who are walking in darkness. But we have to be cleaned up before we can be the beautiful Bride and shining lights in a dark world. So, God works in our lives as the Great Potter, shaping and molding us into the image of his Son who is the Light of the world. The problem is we don't like all the reshaping and cleansing and resist this lesson many times. But learning to persevere in the middle of trials is to learn how to keep on keeping on and not give up.

God has called us to himself for a very special reason. He has a plan and purpose for each one. He has given us gifts which are our tools to carry out his chosen work. This is what life is all about. It isn't about finding a husband or wife, having kids or great friends. We think life should be about happiness and never any kind of trial. Our aim has been to see our kids grow up, mature into good adults, pass the exams and have a successful career. Then later, we can enjoy grand kids and see them grow up too. This is our fulfilled life and if we can help a few people along the way, we are happy about that. And of course, we go to church, hear the gospel preached and grateful to become a child of God. All this is great and God doesn't want to deny us any of these blessings. But if our lives are centered upon these things, we are open to hurt, abuse, bitterness, doubt and anger when things go wrong because they are unexpected. Our happy lives are shattered and we look for somebody to blame.

Usually many Christians turn away from God at this stage because their understanding of what life is all about has been wrong.

People often ask why does God allow suffering. If Christians were treated differently and excused the trials of life, God's Kingdom would be filled with people who were there for the good times only. No one really chooses or wants the trials so everyone would choose to be Christians. We are called to…

*"Come out from among unbelievers, and separate yourselves from them, says the Lord." 2 Corinthians 6:17 NLT*

For every pressure, God's grace is more than sufficient to overcome that need.  In other words, when we feel we can't go on, ask God for a portion of his grace and that will be sufficient to help us go on one more step. Yes, life is definitely hard but remember nothing is going to stop his plan being accomplished in our lives, not even sickness and disease! Remember it's a race we are running and we don't want to be disqualified because we stopped running at the third hurdle. Keep running right through the finishing line.

*"Blessed is the one who perseveres under trial because, having stood the test, that person will receive the crown of life that the Lord has promised to those who love him." James 1:12 NIV*

**PRAYER**

Lord, forgive us when we have stumbled and almost given up. Help us to keep our eyes on Jesus Christ, our Lord and Teacher, and be willing to learn this great lesson of perseverance. Amen.

# AND FINALLY....

*He will not crush the weakest reed or put out a flickering candle.
Finally he will cause justice to be victorious. And his name will be the
hope of all the world.  Matthew 12:20-21 NLT*

I love this verse because certain key words describe our journey.
'Crush....weakest....flickering....Finally....justice....victorious...
.hope'!

One day we will look back over these years of chronic pain and
disease and see how we progressed from being crushed, weak
and hopeless to finally receiving the justice we longed and
prayed for. Complete victory will be ours and what a final and
wonderful hope we will have. It will have been worth all the
persevering and hard painful lessons that brought us closer to
our Lord and helped reshape us more into his image.

There is only one way to victory in the Christian life and that
way is to be willing to give up control. We want to be in charge
of everything that happens and when the control is taken away,
we throw our hands in the air and demand answers to our
questions. It's our old nature trying to work out the
supernatural.

*"If any of you wants to be my follower, you must give up your own
way, take up your cross, and follow me. If you try to hang on to your
life, you will lose it. But if you give up your life for my sake and for the
sake of the Good News, you will save it."  Mark 8:34-35 NLT*

We have been given a heavy cross to carry so God's plan must be amazing! It is certainly much bigger than we imagine. Some of the plan is being worked out in our lives right now preparing us. Not everyone will see the blessings because they refuse to trust God in the furnace of fire. They hold on to complaining and injustice. Every time we complain we are telling our Creator he's got it wrong! Don't give up hope because you can't understand what God is doing. He will use you much more, and your lives will be filled with victory, if you 'let go' the reigns and simply believe God knows what he is doing.

*"Even when there was no reason for hope, Abraham kept hoping—believing that he would become the father of many nations. For God had said to him, "That's how many descendants you will have!" And Abraham's faith did not weaken, even though, at about 100 years of age, he figured his body was as good as dead—and so was Sarah's womb." Romans 4:18-19 NLT*

When the heat of the fire is turned up we feel the intensity of the pain. At these times, we have to choose how to react. The fire reveals all that needs working on and God wants to chip away and mold us more to be like his Son, Jesus Christ. Every trial is planned or allowed by God. He uses everything in our lives and watches carefully how we deal with it. For every trial, there is great blessing both here and in heaven. But we will miss it if we insist on being in control. Don't arrive in heaven just because you believed in Jesus Christ. Arrive walking in victory because you gave Jesus control of this disease and its limitations and unending pain. I have lived long enough to see this spiritual lesson worked out in my own life and the lives of others. Take courage and 'let go'! Victory and blessings wait for us all!

*"All who are victorious will be clothed in white. I will never erase their names from the Book of Life, but I will announce before my Father and his angels that they are mine." Revelation 3:5 NLT*

**PRAYER**

Help us Father to 'let go' and give you control of our lives. We know your plans are beyond our understanding but we want you to mold us to be more like Jesus. We want to live in victory and hope, and praise you every day. Amen.

## NEW BODIES

*And we believers also groan, even though we have the Holy Spirit within us as a foretaste of future glory, for we long for our bodies to be released from sin and suffering. We, too, wait with eager hope for the day when God will give us our full rights as his adopted children, including the new bodies he has promised us. Romans 8:23 NLT*

Wow! What an incredible promise! I can't wait to be in heaven clothed in my new body. No more pain or tears! No more burning! No more nerves trembling! Neurological bladders vanished! No more weakness and painful legs! Can walk or maybe fly! A place where everyone loves and accepts each other…a glorious and perfect place called HOME! Not just an ordinary home but a palace where our majestic King rules and reigns in great splendor. We will be reigning with him if we have loved God, overcome, and lived in victory while on earth. There we will receive our rewards for not giving up and a loving caring God who will wipe away our tears…..

*"He will wipe every tear from their eyes, and there will be no more death or sorrow or crying or pain. All these things are gone forever." Revelation 21:4 NLT*

Imagine living not only in a new perfect body but our feelings will have changed. No more need to persevere, no need to cling on desperately to hope because this new home will be our answer to hope. It will be the fulfillment of all our hopes. Grace will be redundant! We will be like Jesus Christ, perfect in every way. The work of God's grace will have worked itself out in our lives. Learning to trust God in each difficult circumstance will be ended. And the Furnace of Fire will be no more!!

As I look back over my life I see so many apparently negative things God allowed. At the time, it wasn't always easy to see the positive things God wanted to bring out from them. But the older we get so we can look back and see more clearly that God did indeed work all things together for our good. ( Romans 8:28). I needed a lot of refining and the process hurt like crazy. But the more I allowed Father to take control, so I hurt less, had more peace, and most importantly of all, we shared closer fellowship.

As I close this devotional book may I leave this thought with you? When we get to Heaven we will see wonderful and amazing things. We will certainly be enjoying the freedom of new bodies without sickness and disease. It will be absolutely glorious. But God will require us to give an account of how we lived our lives here on earth. So, don't live and react in the moment, live with your eyes fixed firmly on Jesus Christ, trust his plan for you, and live in his abundant grace that will equip you for your every need.

**PRAYER**
Our loving Father, how we look forward to our new bodies free from sickness and pain. We long to be with you in Heaven praising our glorious King. But until that day we rest in the shadow and protection of your wings knowing you are more than sufficient. We love and praise you gracious Lord!  Amen.

## ENCOURAGEMENTS IN THE FURNACE OF FIRE

Why, my soul, are you downcast? Why so disturbed within me? Put your hope in God, for I will yet praise him, my Savior and my God. **Psalms 42:11 NIV**

Do not be afraid, for I have ransomed you. I have called you by name; you are mine. When you go through deep waters, I will be with you. When you go through rivers of difficulty, you will not drown. When you walk through the fire of oppression, you will not be burned up; the flames will not consume you. For I am the Lord, your God, the Holy One of Israel, your Savior......you are honored, and I love you. **Isaiah 43:1-4 NLT**

We are pressed on every side by troubles, but we are not crushed. We are perplexed, but not driven to despair. We are hunted down, but never abandoned by God. We get knocked down, but we are not destroyed. Through suffering, our bodies continue to share in the death of Jesus so that the life of Jesus may also be seen in our bodies. **2 Corinthians 4:8-10 NLT**

He gives power to the weak and strength to the powerless. Even youths will become weak and tired, and young men will fall in exhaustion. But those who trust in the Lord will find new strength. They will soar high on wings like eagles. They will run and not grow weary. They will walk and not faint.
**Isaiah 40:29-31 NLT**

Dear brothers and sisters, when troubles of any kind come your way, consider it an opportunity for great joy. For you know that when your faith is tested, your endurance has a chance to grow. So let it grow, for when your endurance is fully developed, you will be perfect and complete, needing nothing.  **James 1:2-4 NLT**

I wait quietly before God, for my victory comes from him. He alone is my rock and my salvation, my fortress where I will never be shaken.  **Psalms 62:1-2 NLT**

I lie awake thinking of you, meditating on you through the night. Because you are my helper, I sing for joy in the shadow of your wings. I cling to you; your strong right hand holds me securely.  **Psalms 63:6-8 NLT**

Three different times I begged the Lord to take it away. Each time he said, "My grace is all you need. My power works best in weakness." So now I am glad to boast about my weaknesses, so that the power of Christ can work through me. That's why I take pleasure in my weaknesses and in the insults, hardships, persecutions and troubles that I suffer for Christ. For when I am weak, then I am strong.  **2 Corinthians 12:8-10 NLT**

And we know that God causes everything to work together for the good of those who love God and are called according to his purpose for them.  **Romans 8:28 NLT**

Do not be afraid, for I am with you. Don't be discouraged, for I am your God. I will strengthen you and help you. I will hold you up with my victorious right hand.  **Isaiah 41:10 NLT**

The Lord is my shepherd; I have all that I need. He lets me rest in green meadows; he leads me beside peaceful streams. He renews my strength. He guides me along right paths, bringing honor to his name. Even when I walk through the darkest valley, I will not be afraid, for you are close beside me. Your rod and your staff protect and comfort me. You prepare a feast for me in the presence of my enemies. You honor me by anointing my head with oil. My cup overflows with blessings. Surely your goodness and unfailing love will pursue me all the days of my life, and I will live in the house of the Lord forever. **Psalms 23:1-6 NLT**

I will never forget this awful time, as I grieve over my loss. Yet I still dare to hope when I remember this: The faithful love of the Lord never ends! His mercies never cease. Great is his faithfulness; his mercies begin afresh each morning. I say to myself, "The Lord is my inheritance; therefore, I will hope in him!" **Lamentations 3:20-24 NLT**

We can rejoice, too, when we run into problems and trials, for we know that they help us develop endurance. And endurance develops strength of character, and character strengthens our confident hope of salvation. And this hope will not lead to disappointment. For we know how dearly God loves us, because he has given us the Holy Spirit to fill our hearts with his love. **Romans 5:3-5 NLT**

I want to know Christ and experience the mighty power that raised him from the dead. I want to suffer with him, sharing in his death, so that one way or another I will experience the resurrection from the dead! **Philippians 3:10-11 NLT**

Then the Lord answered Job from the whirlwind: "Who is this that questions my wisdom with such ignorant words? Brace yourself like a man, because I have some questions for you, and you must answer them." ...........**Job Chapters 38-42 NIV**

"For I know the plans I have for you," says the Lord. "They are plans for good and not for disaster, to give you a future and a hope." **Jeremiah 29:11 NLT**

So then, since we have a great High Priest who has entered heaven, Jesus the Son of God, let us hold firmly to what we believe. This High Priest of ours understands our weaknesses, for he faced all of the same testings we do, yet he did not sin. So let us come boldly to the throne of our gracious God. There we will receive his mercy, and we will find grace to help us when we need it most. **Hebrews 4:14-16 NLT**

## WHAT HAPPENS NEXT?

Elaine can be contacted at elaine.ballard77@gmail.com

Please don't struggle alone. Join one of the many support groups which will have a good file section on Arachnoiditis. We can educate ourselves from these files and how to live a more fulfilled life, even though it might be different. Dr. Tennant, a formidable and leading Pain Specialist in California, has written many articles and books on Arachnoiditis and has an updated Protocol advising which medicines are helpful as well as suggestions to keep our pain levels more tolerable. Dr. Tennant has helped thousands of patients from around the world to have a better quality of life. All his articles are in these files.

There is hope for us all so don't suffer alone. Together we are stronger and it is amazing how many great friendships are made through these groups.

Elaine is a member of **Arachnoiditis Together We Fight** and sees hundreds of Arachnoiditis patients being helped, supported and encouraged through kind, caring and knowledgeable members. We are a family who pray for each other and give support wherever we can. You will be made very welcome.

Made in United States
North Haven, CT
18 May 2022

19279481R00091